Microsoft Word for the Macintosh Instant Reference

Keystroke Commands

Command	Keystroke Sequence
New	⌘-N
Open	⌘-O
Outline	⌘-Shift-D
Outlining	⌘-U
Page View	⌘-B
Paste	⌘-V
Paragraph	⌘-M
Plain For Style	⌘-Shift-Spacebar
Plain Text	⌘-Shift-Z
Print	⌘-P
Print Preview	⌘-I
Quit	⌘-Q
Repaginate Now	⌘-J
Save	⌘-S
Shadow	⌘-Shift-W
Show ¶/Hide ¶	⌘-Y
Show Ruler/Hide Ruler	⌘-R
Small Caps	⌘-Shift-H
Spelling	⌘-L
Strikethru	⌘-Shift-/
Subscript	⌘-Shift-Hyphen
Superscript	⌘-Shift-=
Symbol Font	⌘-Shift-Q
Underline	⌘-Shift-U
Undo	⌘-Z
Word Underline	⌘-Shift-]

Microsoft® Word for the Macintosh® Instant Reference

Louis Columbus

SYBEX®

San Francisco • Paris • Düsseldorf • Soest

Acquisitions Editor: Dianne King
Developmental Editor: Jim Compton
Copy Editor: Jeff Kapellas
Technical Editor: Celia P. Stevenson
Production Editor: Carolina Montilla
Word Processors: Scott Campbell, Ann Dunn, Susan Trybull
Book Designer: Ingrid Owen
Layout: Suzanne Albertson
Screen Graphics: Cuong Le
Desktop Publishing Production: M.D. Barrera
Proofreader: Bill Cassel
Indexer: Ruthanne Lowe
Cover Designer: Archer Design

Library of Congress Card Number: 91-65776
ISBN: 0-89588-859-9

Manufactured in the United States of America
10 9 8 7 6 5 4 3 2 1

To my wonderful wife Cheryl, who is always a source of inspiration.

Acknowledgments

I greatly appreciate the assistance I received from the editors at SYBEX. Dianne King provided the guidance which made this book possible. Jim Compton made the structure of the manuscript fit the needs of Microsoft Word users. Special thanks to Jeff Kapellas for his great attitude and willingness to work on clarifying the commands in this book. Celia P. Stevenson has provided accurate, timely technical reviews of the manuscript. She shared her extensive knowledge of Microsoft Word and the Macintosh and has made significant contributions to this book. I would also like to give a special note of thanks to (alphabetically) Scott Campbell, Ann Dunn, and Susan Trybull, the SYBEX word processors, for their tireless efforts in incorporating revisions to the manuscript and whose contributions are not to be ignored. At CalComp, John McGowan and Tom Righele provided me with much of their time in order to create the screen graphics. Thank you to Mike Gardner for sharing his Macintosh Lab and knowledge of the Macintosh. Special thanks to Ken Maynard for his support and enthusiasm for this book.

Table of Contents

Introduction

xv

ABOUT MICROSOFT WORD 1
AGAIN 2
BOLD 3
BORDERS 4
CALCULATE 7
CELLS 9
CHANGE 11
CHARACTER 12
CHOOSER 15
CLEAR 17
CLOSE 18
COLUMNS 19
COMMANDS 21
COPY 24
CUT 25
DEFINE STYLES 26
DELETE 28
DOCUMENT 29
EDIT LINK 34
FIND 35
FIND AGAIN 36
FONT 37
FOOTNOTE 39
FORMULA 41

FULL MENUS/SHORT MENUS 46
GLOSSARY 47
GO BACK 50
GO TO 51
HELP 52
HIDE ¶/SHOW ¶ 54
HYPHENATE 56
INDEX 58
INSERT GRAPHICS 59
INSERT INDEX ENTRY 61
INSERT PAGE BREAK 63
INSERT TABLE 64
INSERT TOC ENTRY 66
ITALICS 67
NEW 68
NEW WINDOW 69
OPEN 70
OPEN HEADER/OPEN FOOTER 72
OPEN MAIL 73
OUTLINE 75
OUTLINING 76
PAGE SETUP 80
PAGE VIEW 84
PARAGRAPH 85
PASTE 89
PASTE LINK 90

PLAIN FOR STYLE 92
PLAIN TEXT 93
POSITION 94
PREFERENCES 97
PRINT 100
PRINT MERGE 103
PRINT PREVIEW 106
QUIT 107
RENUMBER 108
REPAGINATE NOW 111
SAVE/SAVE AS 112
SECTION 116
SEND MAIL 120
SHADOW 121
SHOW CLIPBOARD 122
SHOW RULER/HIDE RULER 123
SORT 126
SPELLING 127
STYLES 129
TABLE 131
TABLE OF CONTENTS 133
TABLE TO TEXT 135
UNDERLINE 136
UNDO/REDO 137
UPDATE LINK 138
WORD COUNT 139

Appendix A

Using Microsoft Word on a Network
141

Appendix B

Short Menus versus Full Menus
145

Appendix C

Microsoft Word Command Quick Reference
149

Index

167

Introduction

Finding answers to your questions about Microsoft Word for the Macintosh is now faster and easier than ever before. The *Microsoft Word for the Macintosh Instant Reference* has been carefully researched and organized to assist users of all levels in using the full power of Microsoft Word 4.0. While it does not purport to replace the *Microsoft Word User's Guide*, this book will provide timely answers to your questions about specific commands.

The various Word command references are arranged alphabetically. Each reference provides you with a description of the command and step-by-step instructions for its use. The options for each command are fully explained, and some references provide examples of the command's use. Each command is also cross-referenced with other related commands to guide the reader in locating necessary information.

In addition to the command references, three appendices provide you with useful information on running Microsoft Word on a network and convenient guides to menu options, command keystrokes, and font styles.

Whether you are just learning Word, or are very familiar with its features, you will find the *Microsoft Word for the Macintosh Instant Reference* a useful addition to your computer library.

ABOUT MICROSOFT WORD

• **MENU** Apple

• **DESCRIPTION** The About command displays a dialog box that lists your version of Word and provides you access to Word's online Help system.

To Get Help

1. Open the **Apple** menu.
2. Click on **About Microsoft Word**.
3. The About Microsoft Word dialog box will appear, with a Help button in the upper right corner.
4. Press **Return** or click on the **Help** button to use Word's online Help system.
5. The Help dialog box will appear.
6. Double-click on the topic or command you want to learn about.
7. Select **Cancel** to exit back to the Word desktop.

See Also *Help*

AGAIN

- **MENU** Edit

- **DESCRIPTION** The Again command repeats the preceding command.

To Repeat a Command

1. Modify your document using any command.
2. From the Edit menu, select **Again** (or press **⌘-A**).
3. The preceding command will then be repeated at the cursor's current location.

- **NOTE** The Again command will not repeat a Find command. To repeat a find command, see *Find Again*.

See Also *Find Again, Undo/Redo*

BOLD

• **MENU** Format

• **DESCRIPTION** The Bold command toggles the boldfacing of characters.

To Boldface Text

1. Select the text in your document you want to bold.
2. Open the **Format** menu and select **Bold**, or press **⌘-Shift-B**.
3. The highlighted text in your document will now be bolded.

• **NOTE** You can also create boldface characters by selecting **Bold** before typing the desired text. New text will appear in boldface type. You can turn off the Bold command by selecting **Bold** again or by selecting **Plain Text** (**⌘-Shift-Z**) from the Format menu.

See Also *Define Styles, Styles*

BORDERS

• MENU Format, Paragraph (for paragraphs); Format, Cells (for tables)

• DESCRIPTION The Borders command adds borders to paragraphs and table cells.

To Add Borders to Paragraphs

1. Highlight the paragraphs to be bordered. If you do not specify any paragraphs, your border selections will be applied to any new paragraphs you create.
2. Open the **Format** menu.
3. Select **Paragraph** and click on the **Borders** button. The Paragraph Borders dialog box will appear (Figure 1).
4. Select the border style from the left column.

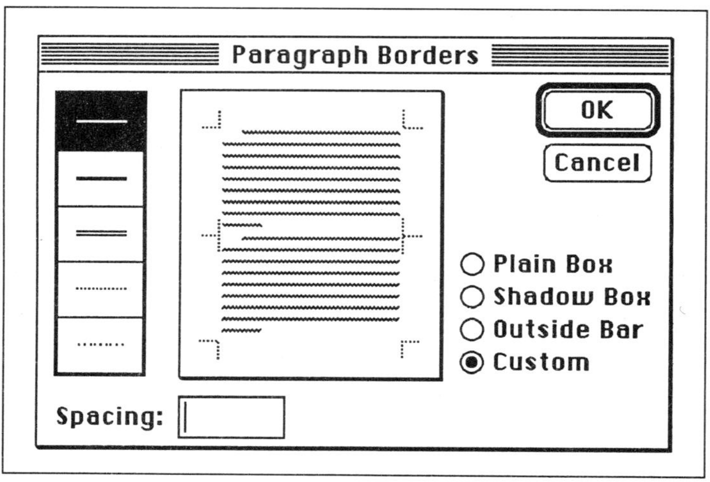

Figure 1: Paragraph Borders dialog box

5. To place a plain or shadow box around the paragraph, click on the appropriate button in the lower right of the dialog box. To place a border along the outside margin only, click on the **Outside Bar** button. Alternatively, you can specify border locations by clicking on or between the appropriate border guides in the center box.

6. To change the amount of space between the border and text, enter a measurement (in points) in the **Spacing** box. The default spacing value is two points. One point equals approximately 1⁄72 inch (.035 cm).

7. Press **Return** twice or click with the mouse on the **OK** buttons in the Borders and Paragraph dialog boxes. To escape without change, click on **Cancel**.

To Add Borders to Cells

1. Use the mouse to select the cells to be bordered.

2. Open the **Format** menu.

3. Choose the **Cells** command.

4. Click on the **Borders** button to display the Cell Borders dialog box (Figure 2).

5. To modify your entire selection of cells as a group, choose the option **Selected Cells As a Block**. If you wish to modify the borders of each individual cell, select **Every Cell In Selection** from the Cell Borders dialog box.

6. Specify the border style to be used by clicking on the appropriate style in the left column. Indicate border placement by clicking on or between the border guides in the right portion of the dialog box.

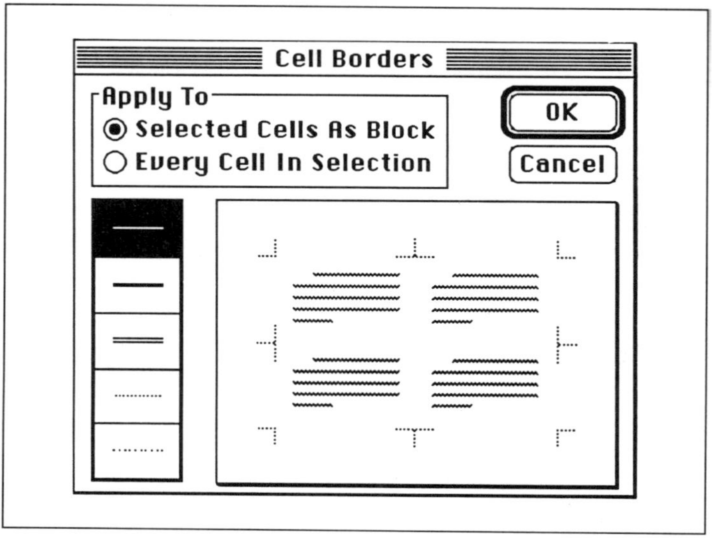

Figure 2: Cell Borders dialog box

7. Press **Return** twice or click on **OK** in the Borders and Cells dialog boxes to apply your selections to the designated cells. Click on **Cancel** to quit the Borders command without change.

• **NOTE** Only PostScript laser printers can print hairline borders. Other printers will print hairline borders as single lines.

See Also *Cells, Paragraph*

CALCULATE

• MENU Utilities (Full Menus only)

• DESCRIPTION The Calculate command offers you a quick and convenient way to perform mathematical operations from within your documents.

To Calculate Numbers

1. Enter the arithmetic expression or column of numbers to be calculated. In your document, precede each number with the appropriate arithmetic symbol (see Notes).
2. Highlight the expression or column with the mouse.
3. Open the **Utilities** menu.
4. Select **Calculate** or press **⌘-=**. The result of your equation will appear in the lower-left corner window and on the Clipboard.
5. Move the insertion point to the place in the document you want to insert the result.
6. Select **Paste** from the Edit menu or press **⌘-V** to paste the results of the equation into your document.

• NOTES Use the following symbols to specify the operations you want completed:

Symbol	Function
*	Multiplication
/	Division
–	Subtraction
+	Addition
%	Percentage

Make sure that the parentheses clearly delineate the calculations you want to complete. Any expressions in parentheses will be completed first.

See Also *Cells*

CELLS

• **MENU** Edit (Full Menus only)

• **DESCRIPTION** The Cells command formats the cells of tables in your document.

To Define Cell Widths

1. Select **Full Menus** from the Edit menu to access the Cells command.
2. Highlight the table or cells to be formatted.
3. Open the **Format** menu.
4. Select the **Cells** command.
5. The Cells command dialog box will appear as shown in Figure 3.

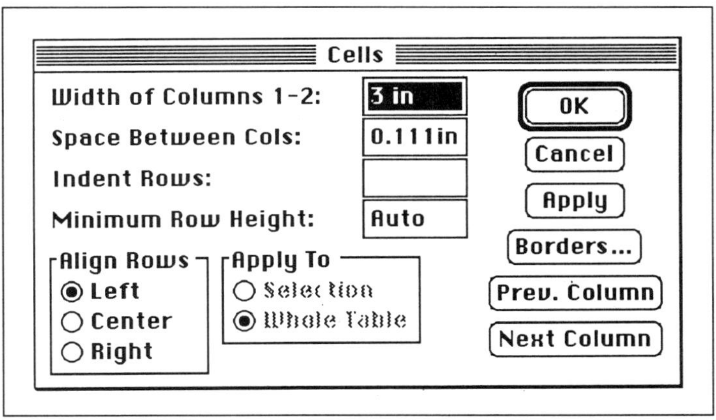

Figure 3: Cells dialog box

6. Format the cells using options described in the Options section below.
7. Click on **OK**, or press **Return**.
8. The cells selected in your document will now reflect the options specified in the Cells dialog box.

Options

Width of Column: Specifies the width of the currently selected column. The default setting will be shown.

Space Between Cols: Sets the amount of space between columns.

Indent Rows: Controls the amount of space between the left margin and the first row.

Minimum Row Height: Defines the height of a row of cells. Type **Auto** to set the minimum height of the cell relative to the tallest character present in a row. User-defined entries may be expressed in points, picas, centimeters, or inches.

Align Rows: Aligns the selected rows on the left indent, right indent, or between the indents specified in the Indent Rows option.

Apply To: Determines whether the entered cell modifications apply only to the selected area, or to the entire table.

Prev. Column: Selects the previous table column and displays its settings.

Next Column: Selects the next table column and displays its settings.

Cancel: Cancels the Cells command and clears all parameters selected in the dialog box. Any changes made with Apply, Prev. Column, or Next Column will not be cancelled.

See Also *Insert Table, Table*

CHANGE

• MENU Utilities

• DESCRIPTION The Change command locates and replaces a specified word or phrase throughout a document or a section of a document.

To Change a Word or Phrase

1. To replace a phrase in only one part of a document, highlight that section of text.
2. Open the **Utilities** menu.
3. Select **Change** or press **⌘-H**.
4. The Change dialog box will appear.
5. Enter the text to be changed and the desired revisions into the **Find What** and **Change To** boxes, respectively. You may instruct Word to search only entire words (not strings of characters embedded in larger words) and exactly match capitalization by clicking on the appropriate boxes.
6. If you want Word to automatically change every occurrence of the specified text, click on **Change All**. If you wish to confirm each individual change, select **Start Search**. If you are making changes in only a portion of the document, the **Change Selection** button will appear instead of the Change All button.
7. If you opted to confirm each change, Word will stop at each occurrence of the word or phrase specified in the Find What box and ask you to verify the change. Select **Change** to confirm, or **Cancel** to end the search.

See Also *Find, Find Again*

CHARACTER

• **MENU** Format (Full Menus only)

• **DESCRIPTION** The Character command provides options for enhancing the appearance of selected text in your documents. With this command, you can control fonts, underlining, character size, text colors, text styles, and character placement.

To Format Characters

1. Select the text to be modified. If no text is selected, then the choices made in the character dialog box will affect only subsequently typed text.
2. Open the **Format** menu.
3. Select the **Character** command or press **⌘-D**. It appears only when the **Full Menus** option has been selected from the Edit menu.
4. The Character dialog box will appear (Figure 4).
5. Modify the text style using the options listed in the Options section below.
6. To view the formatting changes without closing the dialog box, click on **Apply**. To apply the formatting changes and close the Character dialog box, click on **OK** or press **Return**.

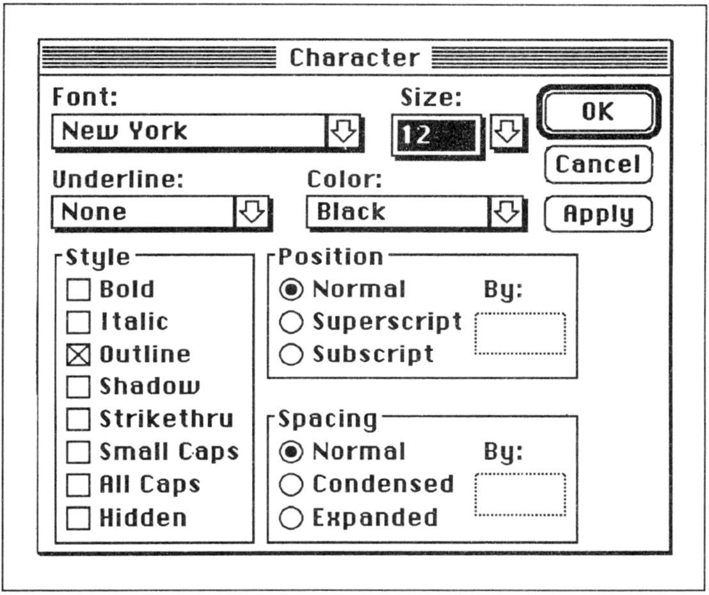

Figure 4: Character dialog box

Options

Font: Initially displays the current font. Once selected, the box presents a list of available fonts. Click on the desired font name.

Size: Initially displays the current text size. Once selected, the box presents a list of available sizes. Click on the desired size.

Underline: Once selected, the box presents a choice of underlining styles: **single**, **double**, or **dotted**. Click on the style you want to use. Select **Word** to underline only words and not spaces.

Color: Initially displays the current color. Once selected, the box presents a list of all available colors. Click on the desired color.

Style: The Style box displays the options that can be used for formatting both upper and lowercase text. Hidden text can also be formatted with this command.

Position: This option controls the position of characters relative to the baseline. Normal places text on the baseline, superscript positions text three points above the baseline, and subscript places text two points below the baseline. You can alter the alignment of superscript and subscript text by entering the desired number of points in the **By** box. One point equals approximately 1⁄72 inch (.035 cm).

Spacing: This option controls the spacing between characters. You can select normal, expanded, or condensed character spacing. The By box specifies the spacing of text in points. For the superscript measurement is 3 points, and 2 points for subscripts.

• NOTES The use of a non-standard font size may produce irregular or jagged print results, depending on your printer.

You can save the text colors within your document on monochrome Macintosh systems. They will print as the colors specified on a color-compatible printer.

See Also *Font*

CHOOSER

• **MENU** Apple

• **DESCRIPTION** The Chooser command is very useful when there are multiple printers available on an AppleTalk network. You can use Chooser to select the printer of your preference.

To Select a Printer

1. Open the **Apple** menu.
2. Select **Chooser**. The Chooser dialog box will appear, as shown in Figure 5.
3. Click on the icon identifying the printer you want to use.
4. If you are using an ImageWriter or compatible printer, choose the port (printer or modem) to which the printer is

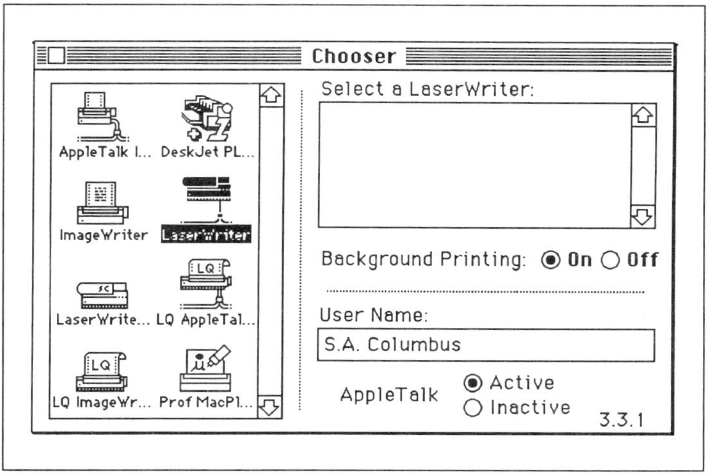

Figure 5: Chooser dialog box (no printer selected)

attached. If you are using a laser printer (such as a Laser-Writer), select the name of the printer in the list box.

5. Click on the AppleTalk **Active** button if you are connected to a network. Type your name in the **User Name** dialog box.

6. Close the Chooser dialog box by clicking on the small box in the upper left corner.

• **NOTES** Be careful to select the correct printer port for your printer. Printing to an external hard disk attached to your modem port may erase the contents of the disk.

In order to facilitate the formatting of your document, select the type of printer you are planning to use prior to specifying the document parameters in the Page Setup dialog box.

If the printer's characteristics do not match the document's parameters, a Page Setup warning box (Figure 6) will appear when you issue a Print command, requesting you to change the document's parameters. Select **Page Setup** from the File menu and revise the document's parameters to conform with the printer's requirements.

See Also *Page Setup, Print*

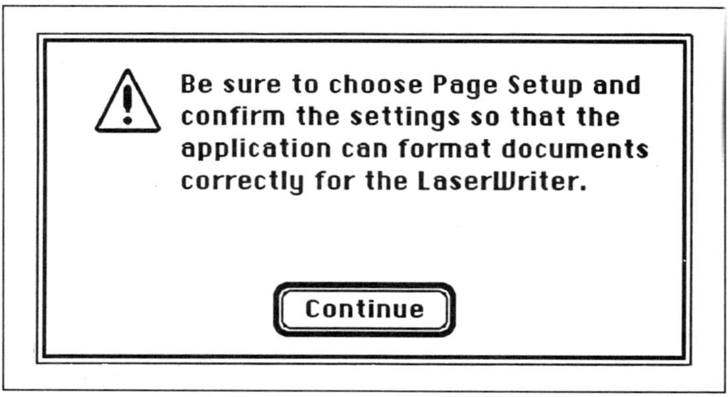

Figure 6: Page Setup warning box

CLEAR

• **MENU** Edit

• **DESCRIPTION** The Clear command deletes selected text without copying it to the Clipboard.

To Remove Text from Documents

1. Use the mouse to select the text you want to delete.
2. Open the **Edit** menu.
3. Choose **Clear**.

• **NOTE** You can also use the Delete and Backspace keys to clear text from your documents.

See Also *Cut, Delete*

CLOSE

• **MENU** File

• **DESCRIPTION** This command closes the currently active document.

To Close a Document

1. Open the **File** menu.
2. Select **Close** or press **⌘-W**.
3. A warning box will appear, prompting you to save your document. If you haven't yet named the document, the Save As dialog box will appear. Type the document name into the **Save As** file window. If your document has already been saved, Word will ask if you want to save your current revisions.
4. Select the options from the Save As dialog box, and press **Enter**. Your document will be saved, and the Word desktop will appear.

See Also *Save/Save As*

COLUMNS

- **MENU** Format, Section

- **DESCRIPTION** The Columns command allows you to create newspaper-style "snaking" columns.

To Create Columns

1. Choose **Section** from the Format menu or press **Option-F14**.
2. Type the number of columns you want on a page in the Numbers box under Columns.
3. In the Spacing box, enter the desired amount of space between columns.
4. Click on **OK** or press **Return**. The text will now re-align itself to match the measurements entered into the dialog box.
5. In order to speed text editing, Word will display columns in "Galley View" (a single, continuous column without headers, footers, or footnotes) when they are first created. To view the columns in their final printed form, select **Page View** from the Document menu, or press **⌘-B** (Figure 7). You can continue to edit text while in the Page View display mode. You can also select **Print Preview** to see the full-page layout of your columns (Figure 8).

See Also *Insert Table, Page View, Print Preview, Section, Table, Table to Text*

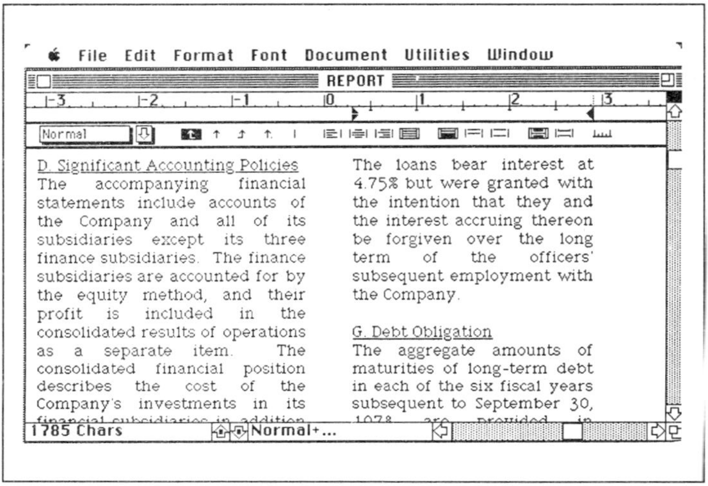

Figure 7: Columns in Page View display.

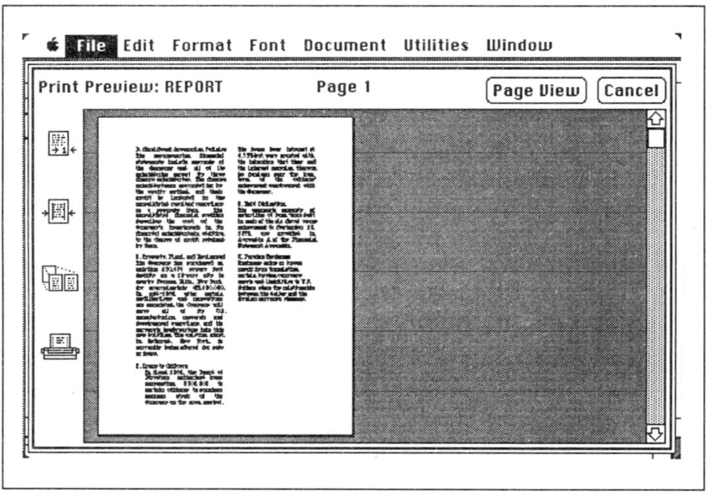

Figure 8: Columns in Print Preview display

COMMANDS

- **MENU** Edit (Full Menus only)

- **DESCRIPTION** The Commands command is a powerful tool for customizing the keystroke and mouse sequences used to access different commands.

To Customize Word Commands

1. If not already selected, select **Full Menus** from the Edit menu.
2. Select **Commands** from the Edit menu.
3. The Commands dialog box will appear (Figure 9).
4. Use the mouse to select a command from the list box located on the left side of the Commands dialog box.
5. Modify the command using the parameters defined in the Options section below.

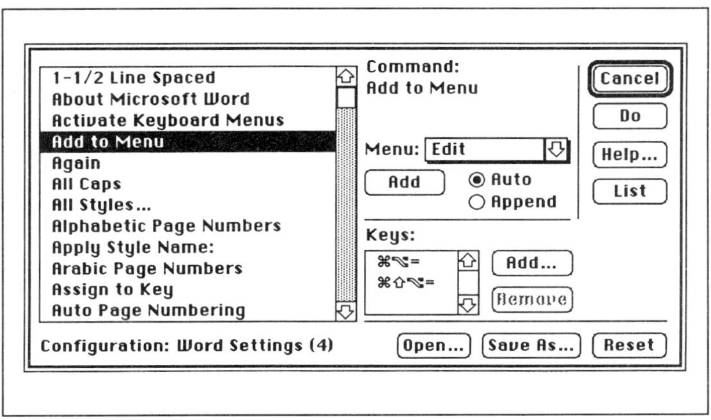

Figure 9: Commands dialog box

Options

Menu: Displays the name of the menu where the selected command can be found. Clicking on the arrow displays a pop-up menu of the other menu titles. To move a command to another menu, select the name of the target menu and click on one of the following buttons:

> **Add:** Adds the highlighted command to the selected menu. If the command is already on the menu, the Add button changes to **Remove**.
>
> **Auto:** Automatically groups the designated command with similar commands on the selected menu.
>
> **Append**: Adds the command to the bottom of the selected menu.

Cancel: Cancels the Commands dialog box but saves the changes made to the command references.

Do: Closes the Commands dialog box and executes the command while updating the current configuration file.

Help: Provides an on-screen definition of the selected command.

List: Creates a list of available commands where the command name is shown in the left column in bold, followed by a description of the command, the menu where it is found, and the keystroke sequence assigned to it. You can sort and print this list using the commands in Word.

Keys: Displays a list of the keystroke sequences, if any, for the selected command. Certain keystrokes appear as symbols in the Keys box:

Symbol	Key
(⌘)	Command
(⌥)	Option
(⇧)	Shift

Symbol	Key
(⌨)	Keyboard
(␣)	Space Bar
(⌤)	Enter

While using the Keys option, you can add or remove keystroke sequences by clicking on the **Add** or **Remove** buttons.

Configuration: Identifies the configuration file for the keystroke sequences being viewed in the Commands dialog box.

Open: Provides a list of configuration files you can open and use. Changes made to the configuration with the Command dialog box are recorded in the active configuration file.

Save As: This option automatically saves the definitions in the Commands dialog box to a new or existing configuration file.

Reset: Changes the current configuration options back either to Word's default values for Full Menus or to the options set prior to the current editing session. Pressing the **Shift** key while clicking on **Reset** sets the values in the configuration file to those specified by Word 4.0 for Full Menus. Pressing the **Option** key while clicking on **Reset** restores the current configuration values to those specified in the previous version of the configuration file.

• NOTES You can get a list of all possible Word commands (over 2000 possible keystroke combinations) by holding down the **Shift** key while clicking on the **List** button.

You can instruct Word to add frequently used document files to your menus. Select **Open File Name** from the Commands list box. An **Open File** button will appear above the Menu box. Click on the button, select the file name from the list box and click on **Add**. Word will create a Work menu containing the document's name. To open the document, click on its name.

See Also *Full Menus/Short Menus, Preferences*

COPY

● **MENU** Edit

● **DESCRIPTION** The Copy command copies selected graphic images or text blocks to the Clipboard. Text blocks copied to the Clipboard will retain their original formatting.

To Copy Text

1. Highlight the text you want to copy to the Clipboard.
2. Open the **Edit** menu.
3. Select **Copy**, or press **⌘-C**.
4. The selected text will be copied to the Clipboard.
5. Move the cursor to the place where you want the text inserted.
6. Use the **Paste** (**⌘-V**) command to insert the text from the Clipboard into the document.

See Also *Cut, Paste*

CUT

- **MENU** Edit

- **DESCRIPTION** The Cut command removes selected graphic items or text blocks from your document. The selected text is moved to the Clipboard along with its formatting for later insertion.

To Remove Text

1. Highlight the graphic item or text block to be removed from the document.
2. Open the **Edit** menu.
3. Select **Cut** or press **⌘-X**.
4. The highlighted text is removed from the document and placed in the Clipboard.
5. Use the **Paste** (**⌘-V**) command to move the text block from the Clipboard to the cursor's location in the document.

See Also *Copy, Paste*

DEFINE STYLES

• **MENU** Format (Full Menus only)

• **DESCRIPTION** The Define Styles command is used to modify style sheets. Style sheets are collections of formatting commands which can be applied to selected characters and paragraphs.

To Modify Style Sheets

1. If not already selected, choose **Full Menus** from the Edit Menu.
2. Open the **Format** menu and select **Define Styles**, or press ⌘-T.
3. The Define Styles dialog box will appear, as shown in Figure 10.

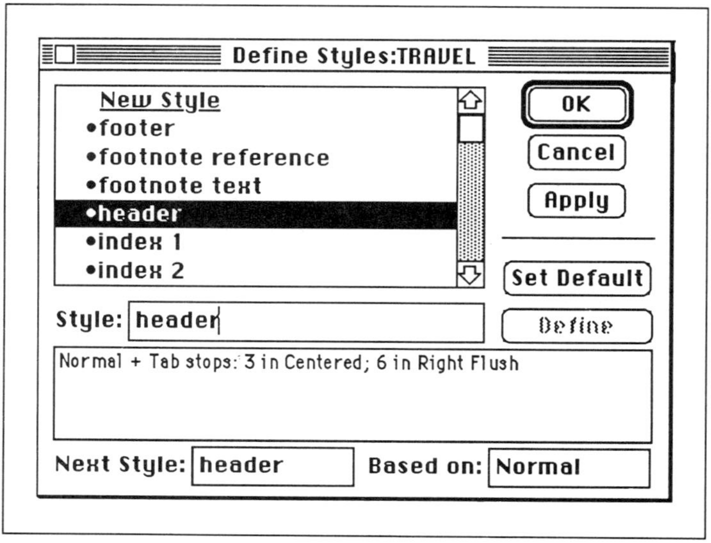

Figure 10: Define Styles dialog box

4. To create a new style, click on **New Style** in the list box. To modify the definition of an existing style, click on the style name.

5. Define your new style in the same manner as you would format text and paragraphs in your document. Open the **Format** menu to access the **Character**, **Paragraph**, **Position**, and text style commands. Open the **Font** menu to select the font name and character size. Your formatting selections will be seen in the box below the Style box.

   If you wish to use an existing style as a guide for your new style, enter the style name in the **Based On** box located in the lower right corner of the Define Styles dialog box.

   To automatically change to another style when you press Return, type the name of the second style in the **Next Style** box.

6. Enter the name of the new style in the **Style** box.

7. To make the selected style the default style, click on **Set Default**.

8. To apply the style to your document without closing the Define Styles dialog box, click on **Apply**. To save the style without applying it to the document, click on **Define**.

9. To apply the style and exit the Define Styles dialog box, click on **OK**. To close the dialog box without discarding the changes you have made with the Apply and Define buttons, click on **Cancel**.

See Also *Character, Font, Paragraph, Position, Styles*

DELETE

• **MENU** File (Full Menus only)

• **DESCRIPTION** The Delete Command removes document files from your hard disk or floppy diskettes.

To Delete a File

1. Make sure that the **Full Menus** option is selected in the Edit menu.
2. Open the **File** menu and select **Delete**.
3. The Delete Document dialog box will appear.
4. Select the file you want to delete by clicking on its name in the list box located on the left side of the dialog box. If the file is not shown in the list box, click on the **Drive** button to select another disk drive, or change the floppy diskette by clicking on the **Eject** button. (*Note:* If you have installed System 7 on your Macintosh, the **Drive** button will be labelled **Desktop**.)
5. Click on the **Delete** button to remove the file from the disk. A message box will appear asking you to confirm that you want to delete the file. Click on **Yes**, the Delete dialog box will close, and your file will be deleted.

DOCUMENT

● **MENU** Format

● **DESCRIPTION** The Document command defines the left, right, top and bottom margins for your documents. If used in the Full Menus mode, it will also control odd or even margin adjustments, footnote positioning, and tab stop locations.

To Set Margins and Document Options

1. Open the **Format** menu and select **Document**, or press ⌘-**F14**. If **Short Menus** has been selected from the Edit menu, the Document dialog box will appear, as shown in Figure 11. If Word is in **Full Menus** mode, the full Document dialog box will appear (Figure 12).

2. Enter the desired options, listed below. Options other than **Margins** are available only in the Full Menus mode.

Margins: Sets the width of the top, bottom, left and right margins. Use the Preferences command to define the unit of measure (inches, centimeters, points or picas).

Mirror Even/Odd Margins: The Mirror Even/Odd Margins option sets the document's margins for binding in book format. The left margins of the odd-numbered pages in your

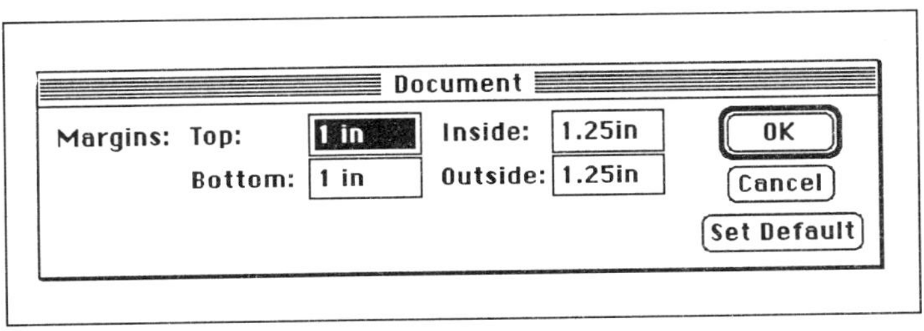

Figure 11: Document Command dialog box: Short Menus

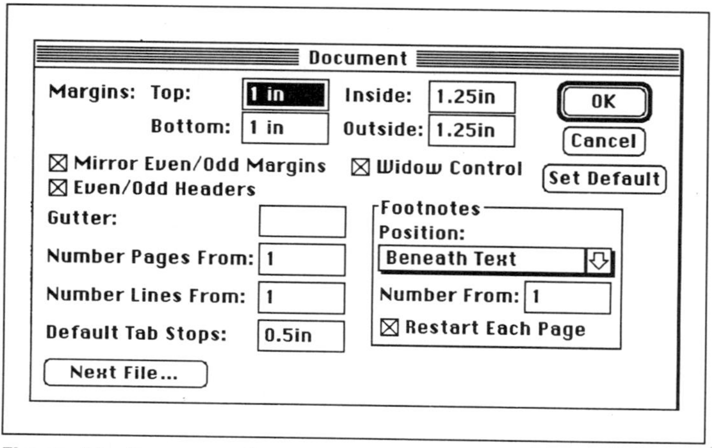

Figure 12: Document Command dialog box: Full Menus

document (the right-side pages in a book) and the right margins of the even-numbered (left-side) pages are increased to provide more room for binding.

Even/Odd Headers: Selecting this option displays either the Open Even Header or the Open Odd Header window, depending on your cursor's location. You may type separate headers for the odd and even pages in your document. (*Note:* The Section dialog box includes a Page Numbering option for specifying the position and style used for page numbers in headers and footers. For more information, see the *Section* command reference.)

Gutter: A "gutter" is extra space allocated to the left and right margins in a document to facilitate binding. Selecting the Gutter option will increase the left margin of odd numbered pages and the right margin of even-numbered pages.

Number Pages From: Sets the starting page number for your document. If the document is linked to another with a Next File option, enter 0 in this box.

Number Lines From: Specifies the number from which you want to number lines in your document. Use the Number Lines From option to create sequential numbered line references throughout a series of documents.

Default Tab Stops: Sets the default tab stops used by Word.

Next File: Select this option to define the next file to be used by Word in creating an index or table of contents. The Next File option can also be used to create a print queue of related documents to be printed sequentially upon the issuance of a Print command.

Widow Control: Select this option to ensure that single lines are kept together with their paragraphs. De-selecting this option will cause Word to print as many lines as possible on a single page, regardless of paragraph breaks.

Footnotes: Clicking the mouse button on the down arrow of this option will display a list of alternative footnote positions. You may choose to place footnotes at the bottom of the page, directly beneath the footnoted text, at the end of the text section (as defined by a section mark), or at the end of the document.

Number From: Specifies the first number to be used for numbering footnotes in your document.

Restart Each Section: Selecting this command will cause Word to restart the numbering of footnotes on each page, if either the Bottom of Page or Beneath Text footnote options is selected, or at the end of each section, for the End of Section footnote option.

Set Default: This option saves the current Document dialog box settings as the default. Any new documents you create will use these settings.

3. To apply the changes made in the Document dialog box to your document, press **Return**, or click on **OK**. To close the dialog box without applying or saving the changes, click on **Cancel**.

• EXAMPLE One of the features which the Document dialog box controls is footnote placement. Figure 13 shows the document titled "OVERVIEW" after a Print Preview command. Note the position of the footnote at the bottom of page one.

At a later point in time, the author decided to change the position of the footnote and place it at the end of its section in the document. To do this, the author opened the Document dialog box, clicked on the arrow in the Footnotes box to open the drop-down menu, and dragged the mouse to highlight the End of Section option (Figure 14).

The footnote then moved to the designated end of the section. Note the footnote's new position in Figure 15.

See Also *Commands, Footnote, Page View, Preferences, Print Preview, Section*

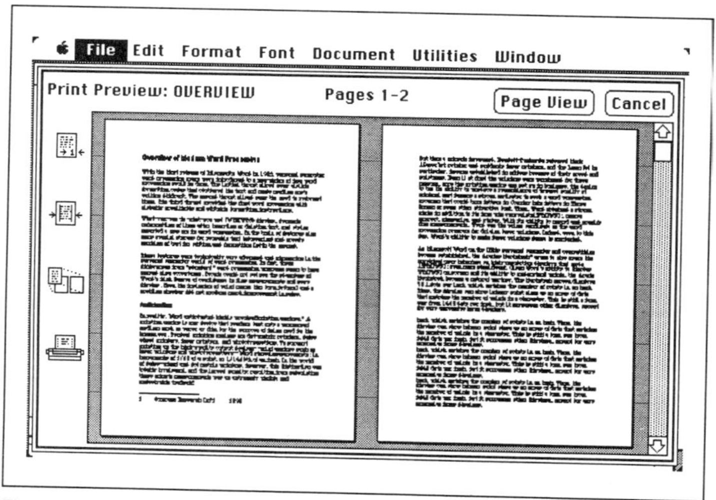

Figure 13: Document in Print Preview mode

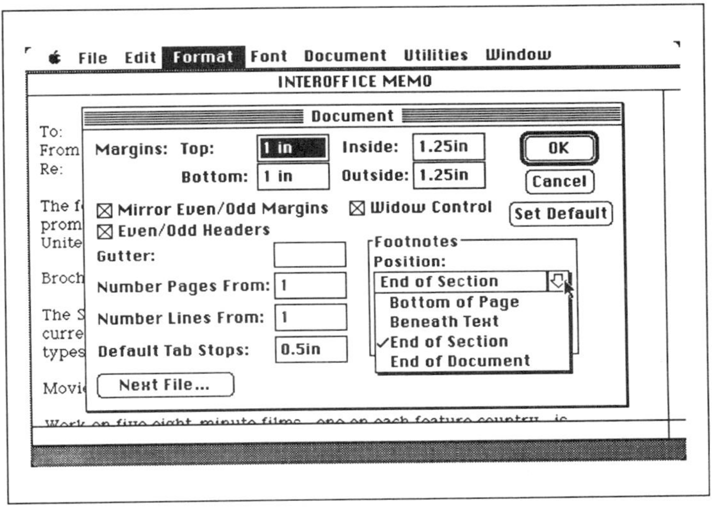

Figure 14: Selection of the End of Section option

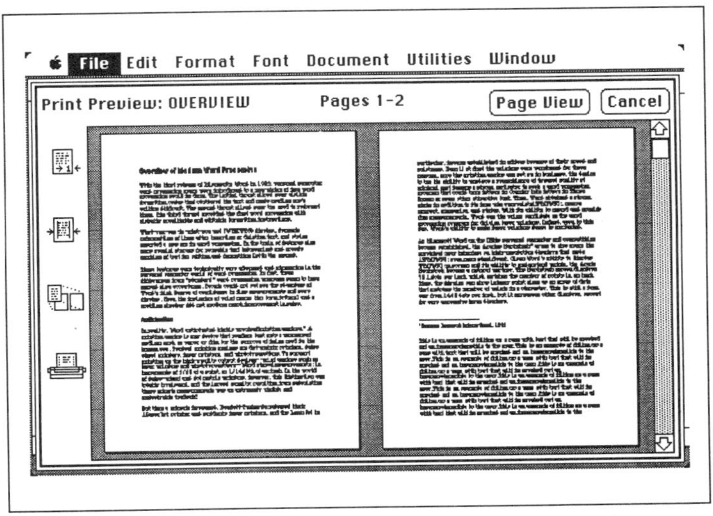

Figure 15: Document after revision (Print Preview mode)

EDIT LINK

• **MENU** Edit (Full Menus only)

• **DESCRIPTION** The Edit Link command allows you to directly access and revise information from other applications linked to your Microsoft Word document.

To Edit Linked Files

1. If necessary, select **Full Menus** from the Edit menu.
2. Highlight the information you want to update in your Microsoft Word document.
3. Open the **Edit** menu.
4. Press the **Shift** key and select **Edit Link**.
5. The application linked to your document will be launched and the file linked to your Word document will appear. If the linked file is not found, a dialog box will appear as-king you for assistance in locating the file.
6. Use the linked application to modify the data.
7. To insert the revised data into your document, press **⌘-,** (comma). If you do not want to add the new data to your document, use the MultiFinder to switch back to Microsoft Word.

See Also *Paste Link, Update Link*

FIND

- **MENU** Utilities

- **DESCRIPTION** The Find command locates specific words or text strings in your documents.

To Find Specific Words or Strings

1. Open the **Utilites** menu and select **Find**, or press **⌘-F**. The Find dialog box will appear.
2. Type the word or text string to be searched in the **Find What** box. Click on the **Whole Word** box to search only entire words and not embedded text. Click on the **Match Upper/Lowercase** box to search only for text which exactly matches the capitalization of the text in the Find What box.
3. Click on the **Start Search** button, or press **Return**.
4. As the words or phrases you are searching for are encountered, the Start Search button will change to Find Next until all occurrences are found.
5. When you have finished your search, close the dialog box by clicking on the small box in the upper left hand corner or by clicking on **Cancel**.

See Also *Find Again*

FIND AGAIN

• **MENU** Utilities

• **DESCRIPTION** The Find Again command continues a search for the last entry made in the Find What box of the Find command. This feature can be useful when you are editing several documents that will comprise a larger manuscript.

To Continue a Search

1. Open the **Utilities** menu and select **Find Again** or press **⌘-Option-A**.
2. Word will begin searching for the text string entered in the Find dialog box. The box will not reappear.
3. The next occurrence of the text string will appear highlighted on your screen. Press **⌘-Option-A** to continue searching the document for new occurrences of the string.

See Also *Find*

FONT

• DESCRIPTION The Font menu provides a list of the various character styles (fonts) and sizes available for use in your document.

To Change Font Sizes

1. If you wish to alter the appearance of a specific body of text, highlight that text with the mouse.
2. Open the **Font** menu. By holding down the mouse button, you can see a complete listing of the available fonts and font sizes (Figure 16). The currently selected font and size will be marked with checks (✓).
3. Move the mouse down the list, releasing the button when you reach the font or size you want to use.

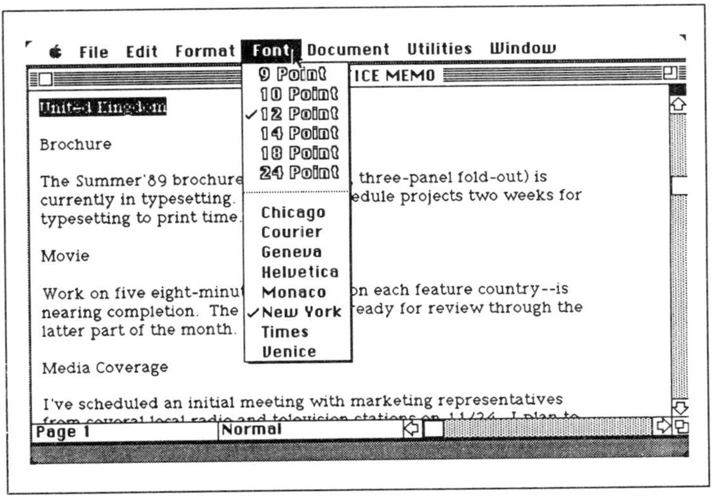

Figure 16: Font menu

4. The selection you have made will be reverse-highlighted for a moment, and then the Font menu will disappear from the screen.

5. The selected text will now change to the new font and size. If you did not specify a body of text to be changed, any subsequently entered text will appear in the new font and size.

See Also *Character, Preferences*

FOOTNOTE

• **MENU** Document

• **DESCRIPTION** The Footnote command adds footnotes to your documents. You can also use the command to define the note numbering style in terms of sequential numbers, asterisks (*), or daggers (†). The available features of the Footnote command vary depending on whether the Short Menus or Full Menus option is selected.

To Add a Footnote to Your Document

1. Open the **Document** menu and select **Footnote**, or press ⌘-E.
2. The Footnote dialog box will appear as shown in Figure 17. Additional options are available in the Footnote dialog box when the Full Menus option is selected (Figure 18).
3. You may choose to have Word automatically number your notes in sequence by clicking on the **Auto-numbered Reference** box. Alternatively, you can enter the footnote symbol of your choice in the **Footnote Reference Mark** box.
4. In the Full Menus mode, you can modify the separator between the text and footnotes by clicking on the **Separator** button. By clicking on the **Cont. Separator** button, you can revise the separator used for notes continued from the previous page. Clicking on the **Cont. Notice** button allows you to create a tag line (such as *Continued on next page*) for notes continued on another page.
5. Once you have set the options you prefer, click on **OK**, or press **Return**. Your footnote selections will be added to your document.

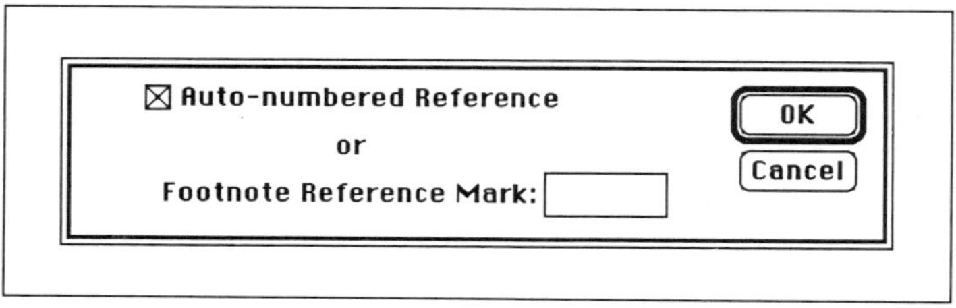

Figure 17: Footnote dialog box: Short Menus

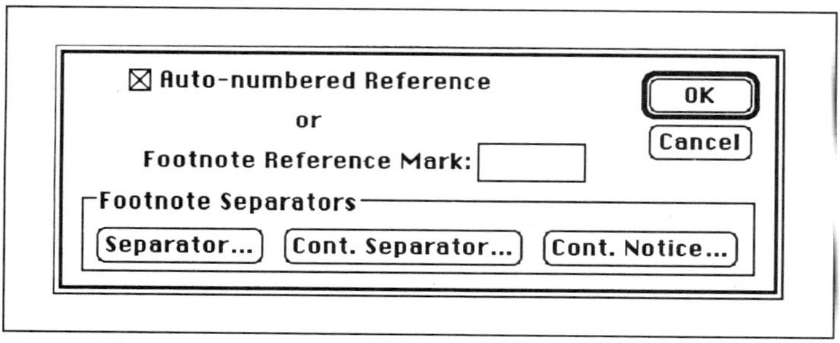

Figure 18: Footnote dialog box: Full Menus

FORMULA

• MENU See *Notes*

• DESCRIPTION The Formula command is a powerful equation editor. You can use it to create, edit and view complex mathematical expressions in your documents. You must install the Symbol character set (available from Apple) on your Macintosh in order to use the Formula command.

To Create Mathematical Formulas

1. Make sure that the **Full Menus** option is selected in the Edit menu.
2. From the Edit menu select Show ¶. You can also use the keyboard shortcut **⌘ - Y** to switch between the Show ¶/Hide ¶ views of your document.
3. Press **⌘-Option-** to signal to Word that you will be entering a formula.
4. Enter the desired formula commands and options. The format Word uses for formula commands is .*command*.*option* (*argument*), where .\\ is the screen representation of **⌘-Option-**.
5. Select **Hide ¶** to view the formula in its printed form.

Formula Commands and Options

Array .\\A (*values*) This option defines a two-dimensional columnar array of values. Use parentheses to surround the list of numbers to be included in the array and delineate the numbers with commas. You can place any number of integers in the array, listing them in the values section in row-wise order.

You may use the following options when formatting arrays:

.\AL	Aligns values along the left side of the columns.
.\AR	Aligns values along the right side of the columns.
.\AC	Centers values within the columns.
.\CO*n*	Specifies the number of columns (*n*) in the array. Word uses one column as the default value.
.\VS*n*	Sets the vertical spacing to *n* number of points.
.\HS*n*	Sets the horizontal spacing to *n* number of points.

Bracket .\B.*option(expression)* This option places a selected character around the indicated expression. You can use the following options with Bracket:

.\BC.*c*	Places the character *c* on both sides of the indicated expression.
.\LC.*c*	Places the character *c* on the left side of the indicated expression.
.\RC.*c*	Places the charater *c* on the right side of the indicated expression.

Displace .\D.*option expression* This option sets the position of the following expression relative to the first column location of the formula. Distance is measured in points. (One point equals approximately 1⁄72 inch.) You can use the following options with Displace:

.\BA*n*()	Moves back *n* points and overstrikes characters.
.\FO*n*()	Moves forward *n* points from the immediately preceding character on the text line.
.\LI	Inserts a line from the end of the preceding character to the beginning of the next character.

Note that you must insert the parentheses following the Displace options.

Fraction .\F (*numerator, denominator*) Defines a fraction within a formula, or standing alone in the text. The numerator and denominator can include numbers, formulas, letters, or text.

For example:

.\F((Y=A+Bx),(A=Y-Bx))

results in:

$$\frac{(Y=A+Bx)}{(A=Y-Bx)}$$

Integral .\I (*lowerlimit, upperlimit, integrand*) This option creates the symbol for an integral operation. Use the following options to define the integral:

.\FC*c*	Fixes the height of the operator *c*.
.\IN	Defines and displays an inline format of the equation with the limits displayed on the same line as the integral symbol.
.\PR	Creates a pi (π) symbol.
.\SU	Creates a sigma (Σ) symbol.
.\VC.*c*	Varies the height of operator *c* to match that of the integrand (the third option argument).

For example:

.\IN.\SU(i=5,x,r)

results in

$$\sum_{i=5}^{x} r$$

List .\L (*values*) This option identifies the members of a string as a single list. This is very convenient when the numerator and denominator of a fraction contain a series of elements.

For example:

.F\(.\L(2,3,3,9,25),.\L(5,6,8,42))

results in

$$\frac{3,12,32,100}{7,9,13,31,47}$$

Overstrike .\O (*characters*) This command overlays a series of characters upon each other. For example, type **.\O(0,/)** to create a slashed zero (ø).

You may use the following options with Overstrike:

- .\AC Centers the equation or letter in the middle of a monospaced area used by the overstrike feature to isolate characters.
- .\AL Aligns the first strike-out character to the left edge of the area.
- .\AR Aligns the first strike-out character to the right edge of the area.

Because font widths vary, you may need to experiment with the various overstrike options to achieve the results you want.

Radical .\R (*root integer*) This option creates a radical (root) sign. If you enter only a single number, the number command will produce the symbol for the square root ($\sqrt{\ }$) of that number. If you enter more than one number, the first will appear as the index of the radical.

For example, typing .\R(14,256) will generate $\sqrt[14]{256}$.

Superscript/Subscript .\S (values) This command creates super and subscripts. Word automatically positions the argument 3 points above or below the current baseline. Word stacks the values in the order listed. For example, R.\S(1,4) results in R^{1}_{4}.

You may use the following options:

- .\AI*n* Sets the space above the text baseline to *n* number of points.
- .\DI*n* Sets the space below the text baseline to *n* number of points.
- .\DO*n* Positions the subscript *n* points below the text baseline.
- .\UP*n* Positions the superscript *n* points above the baseline.

Box .\X (*expression*) This command encloses the expression in a box. You can use the following option to control the appearance of the box:

.\BO	Draws the bottom border of the box.
.\LE	Draws the left border of the box.
.\RI	Draws the right border of the box.
.\TO	Draws the top border of the box.

For example, .\X.\LE.\RI(1500) will result in |1500|

If no options are specified, Word will automatically draw the entire box.

• NOTES In order to use the Formula command, the Symbol character set must be installed on your Macintosh. Use the Font/DA mover to install the Symbol character set. If you do not have the Symbol character set, contact an Apple dealer.

Note that the Formula command is activated only by a keyboard command (**⌘-Option-**) and does not appear on the menus.

See Also *Hide ¶/Show ¶*

FULL MENUS/ SHORT MENUS

- **MENU** Edit

- **DESCRIPTION** The Full Menus option displays the complete list of Word commands on the menus. Selecting Short Menus causes Word to display only the most basic editing and printing commands.

To Select Full Menus

1. Open the **Edit** menu and select **Full Menus**.
2. The Word desktop will then display the complete set of commands in each pull-down menu.
3. To return to short menus, select **Short Menus** from the Edit menu.

- **NOTE** Word selects Short Menus as the default on start-up.

See Also *Preferences; Appendix B: Short Menus versus Full Menus.*

GLOSSARY

- **MENU** Edit (Full Menus only)

- **DESCRIPTION** The Glossary command can be used to store and retrieve frequently used words, phrases, or graphics. You can think of the Glossary command as an insert library for your documents. You can print the contents of a glossary for future reference.

To Create a Glossary Entry

1. If not already selected, select **Full Menus** from the Edit menu.
2. Highlight the text or graphic image that you want to add to the glossary.
3. Open the **Edit** menu and select **Glossary** or press **⌘-K**. The Glossary dialog box will appear, as shown in Figure 19.
4. The list box on the left side of the Glossary dialog box displays the names of current glossary entries. Note that

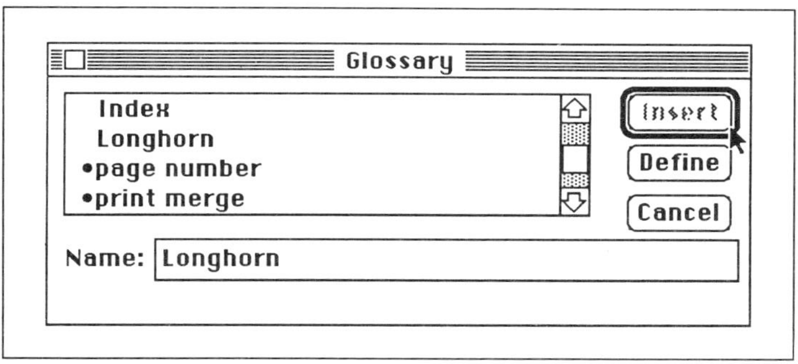

Figure 19: Glossary dialog box

Microsoft provides you with entries for placing the current date and time in your documents.

5. To include your selection in the glossary, click on **New** and type the name for that glossary entry in the **Name** box. If you wish to replace an existing entry with your selection, click on the existing entry's name.

6. Click on **Define** to save your new glossary entry. The name of the glossary entry will now appear in the list box.

7. To save the revised glossary as a separate, personalized glossary, select **Save As** from the File menu. Type the name of the revised glossary in the **Save Current Glossary** box and click on **Save**. If you opt not to create a new glossary, all new entries and revisions will be saved in the default Standard Glossary.

8. To close the Glossary dialog box, click on **Cancel** or on the small box located in the upper left corner of the dialog box.

To Insert a Glossary Entry into a Document

1. If not already selected, select **Full Menus** from the Edit menu.

2. Move the cursor to the point where you wish to insert the glossary entry.

3. Open the **Edit** menu and select **Glossary**, or press **⌘-K**. The Glossary dialog box will appear, as shown in Figure 19.

4. Word displays the Standard Glossary by default. To use a personalized glossary, open the **File** menu, select **Open**, and open the glossary in the same manner as you would a document file.

5. Click on the name of the desired glossary entry in the Glossary command list box. The contents of the selected glossary entry will appear below the Name box.

6. Select **Insert**. The text, phrase, or graphic image will be inserted at the cursor's location in your document.

7. To close the Glossary dialog box, click on **Cancel** or in the box located in the upper left corner of the dialog box.

• **NOTE** To print the contents of your Glossary, first open the Glossary dialog box, then select **Print** from the File menu or press **⌘-P**.

See Also *Print, Save/Save As*

GO BACK

• **MENU** Utilities (Full Menus only)

• **DESCRIPTION** The Go Back command moves the cursor to a preceding selection or insertion point (of up to three previous places) and then returns the cursor to its original location.

To Move to a Prior Insertion Point

1. If not already selected, select **Full Menus** from the Edit menu.
2. Open the **Utilities** menu and select **Go Back**, or press **⌘-Option-Z**.
3. The cursor will return to the previous section or insertion point. Repeating the command will move the cursor to the next prior insertion point (up to three previous points) and then back to the cursor's original position.

• **NOTE** The 0 (zero) key on the numeric keypad also performs the Go Back command when the Number Lock is toggled off.

See Also *Copy, Cut, Paste*

GO TO

- **MENU** Utilities

- **DESCRIPTION** The Go To command allows you to move quickly to different pages in your document.

To Move to a Specific Document Page

1. Open the **Utilities** menu and select **Go To**, or press **⌘-G**.
2. The Go To dialog box will appear.
3. Type the number of the page to which you want to move, then press **Return** or click on **OK**.
4. The cursor will move to the top of the selected page.

- **NOTES** You can also access the Go To dialog box by double-clicking on the page number area in the lower left corner of the screen.

Specifying a page number greater than the length of your document will automatically position the cursor at the final page of your document.

See Also *Find, Find Again*

HELP

• MENU Window

• DESCRIPTION The Help command provides you with information on specific commands and tasks in Microsoft Word.

To Access Word's Online Help System

1. Open the **Utilities** menu and select **Help**.
2. The Help dialog box will appear as shown in Figure 20. On the left side of the dialog box is a list box of subjects included in Word's online help system.
3. Select the desired subject by double-clicking on the subject's name, or by clicking once each on the subject's name and the **Help** button. The list box will change into a scrolling window containing information on the topic and page references to the *Microsoft Word User's Guide* (Figure 21).
4. To view the previous or following help topic, click on **Previous** or **Next**. To return to the topic list, click on the **Topics** button, or press **Return**.
5. To exit the Help system, click on **Cancel**.

• NOTE You can also access Word's help system by pressing **⌘-?**. The mouse pointer will turn into a question mark (**?**). Selecting a menu command with this pointer will open the Help dialog box and display the help information for that command. You can then move around in or exit the Help system as described above.

See Also *About Microsoft Word*

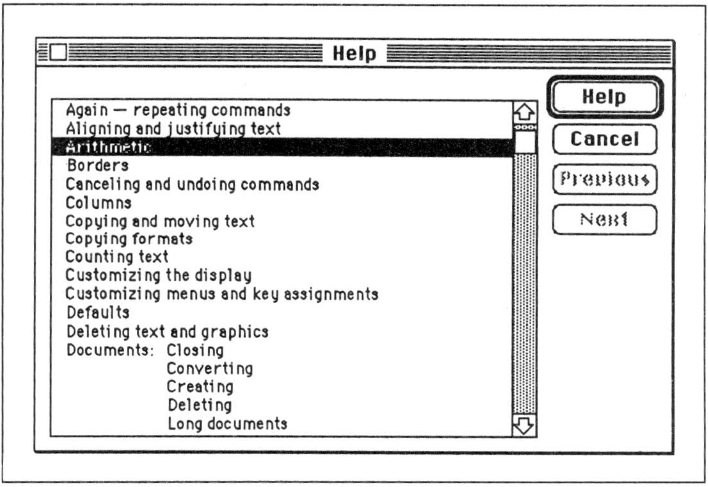

Figure 20: Help dialog box

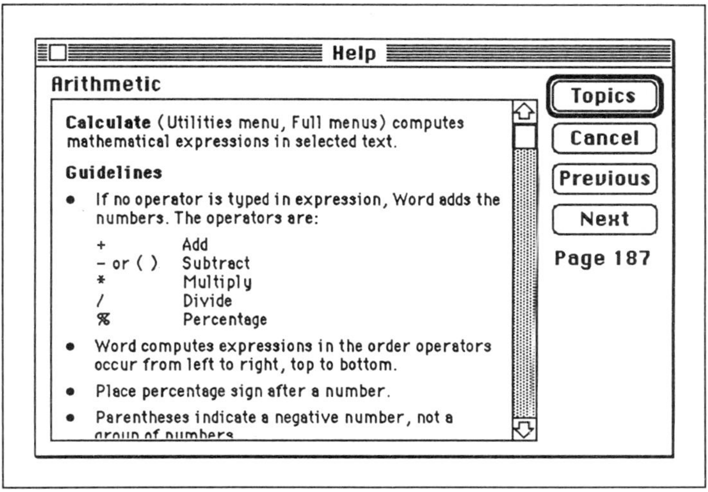

Figure 21: A Help screen

HIDE ¶/SHOW ¶

• **MENU** Edit

• **DESCRIPTION** The Hide ¶/Show ¶ command toggles the display of special characters and delimiters in your documents. Hide ¶ also displays mathematical formulas (created by the Formulas command) in their final printed form.

To Hide/Show Special Characters

1. Open the **Edit** menu.
2. Select **Show ¶** or press **⌘-Y**.
3. The special characters used to define different items in your document will now be visible on your Macintosh screen.
4. To hide the special characters, select **Hide ¶** on the Edit menu, or press **⌘-Y**.

The following special characters are viewable with the Show ¶ command:

Function	Symbol
Paragraph	¶
End-of-line mark	↵
Normal space	. . .
Nonbreaking space	~ ~ ~
Tab mark	➧
Normal hyphen	– – –
Nonbreaking hyphen	~~~
Optional hyphen	⸗ ⸗ ⸗

Function	Symbol
Formula character	.\
Graphic frame	
Page number	3
Date	5/11/91
Time	12:05 PM
Auto-numbered footnote reference mark	2
End-of-cell mark	•
Paragraph properties mark	■

• **NOTE** Word automatically enters Hide ¶ mode at start-up.

See Also *Formulas*

HYPHENATE

• **MENU** Utilities (Full Menus only)

• **DESCRIPTION** The Hyphenate command allows you to view, modify, and designate hyphenation points for words located at the end of a line.

To Hyphenate Characters

1. When you are creating or editing your document, you may specify one of three types of hyphenation.

   Normal Hyphenation: Press the dash (-) key for terms with visible hyphens, such as, "two-piece."

   Optional Hyphenation: Press ⌘- (dash) to indicate an optional hyphenation point (¬) within a word. This hyphen is visible only when the Show ¶ view is selected. Word will break the word at this point if it is at the end of a line.

   Nonbreaking Hyphenation: Press ⌘-~ (tilde) to hyphenate a word you don't want broken. For example, the name "Jameson-Greene" would always appear as a single word when joined with a nonbreaking hyphen (⁻).

2. If not already selected, select **Full Menus** from the Edit menu.
3. Open the **Utilities** menu and select **Hyphenate**.
4. The Hyphenate dialog box will appear.
5. If you want to hyphenate capitalized words, click on the **Hyphenate Capitalized Words** box.
6. To automatically hyphenate all the words in your document, select **Hyphenate All**. If you have highlighted a specific portion of your text, the **Hyphenate All** button changes to **Hyphenate Selection**.

7. Select **Start Hyphenation**. As the Hyphenation command scans your document, it will encounter words that it will suggest be hyphenated. Suggested hyphenation points will be shown in the Hyphenate box. A vertical dotted line indicates the point where the right margin intersects the word.

8. You can modify the hyphenation points within words by moving the cursor to the desired location and entering the type of hyphenation you prefer.

9. If you accept the proposed hyphenation, click on **Change**. The word will be changed and re-inserted into the document. If you reject the suggested hyphenation, click on **No Change**.

10. To exit the Hyphenation dialog box, click on **Cancel**.

• **NOTE** Use the Hyphenate command after you complete the editing of a document but prior to its repagination and printing in order to get a better idea of how your final printed document will look. Also, rehyphenate your document whenever you change the typeface, font size, margins, or lengthen a line of text.

See Also *Change, Find, Hide ¶/Show ¶*

INDEX

• MENU Utilities (Full Menus only)

• DESCRIPTION The Index command is used to create an index of items appearing in your document.

To Create an Index

1. If not already selected, select **Full Menus** from the Edit menu.
2. Open the **Utilities** menu.
3. Select **Index**.
4. The Index dialog box will appear. Choose the appropriate parameters for the index, as listed below:

   Format: Select the **Nested** option to place index sub-entries below and to the right of main entries. Select **Run-in** to place index sub-entries on the same line as main entries.

   Index Characters: Select **All** to index your entire document at once. The index created will appear at the end of your document. To speed indexing in larger documents, you may specify a range of letters for indexing by entering the appropriate letters in the **From** and **To** boxes.
5. To exit without creating an index, click on **Cancel**. Otherwise, select **Start**. The index for your document will begin to be created. When the index is completed, it will be added to the end of your document.

See Also *Find, Insert Index Entry*

INSERT GRAPHICS

• **MENU** Document (Full Menus only)

• **DESCRIPTION** The Insert Graphics command creates a graphic frame which allows you to paste graphic images into your document.

To Insert Graphics into Your Document

1. If MultiFinder is available on your Macintosh system, select it to facilitate movement between your graphics program and Microsoft Word.
2. Use your graphics program to create the image you want to insert into your document.
3. Select **Copy** or **Cut** to transfer the image to the Clipboard. Certain graphics programs do not have Clipboard support. If the Clipboard is not available, save the graphic image to the Scrapbook. For additional information on using the Scrapbook, see your Apple Macintosh user's manual.
4. Using MultiFinder, switch to Microsoft Word. If your Macintosh does not have MultiFinder, quit from your graphics program, and then launch Microsoft Word.
5. Open your Word document file and move the cursor to the location you wish to insert the graphic image.
6. Insert a graphic frame into the document by opening the **Document** menu and selecting **Insert Graphics**.
7. Click on the graphic frame, then open the **Edit** menu and select **Paste**, or press **⌘-V**. The graphic image will appear in the graphic frame.
8. You can re-size the graphic frame by first clicking on it with your mouse. A series of handles will appear in the

bottom right portion of the frame. Use these handles to scale or crop your graphic image. To scale the graphic, press the **Shift** key and drag one of the handles to the desired location. To crop or enlarge the frame, drag the handle towards the interior or exterior of the box.

• **NOTE** The Insert Graphics command places an open graphic frame at the cursor's location in your document. The graphics frame can be bolded, shadowed, outlined, or underlined in the same manner as an alphabetic character. Graphic frames can also be duplicated to create a series of check boxes or a grid by pressing **⌘-D**.

See Also *Copy, Cut, Paragraph, Paste, Position*

INSERT INDEX ENTRY

• **MENU** Document (Full Menus only)

• **DESCRIPTION** The Insert Index Entry command marks words or phrases for entry into an index.

To Mark an Index Entry

1. If not already chosen, select **Full Menus** from the Edit menu.
2. You can either mark text within your document for later inclusion in an index, or compile an index while you are creating your document.
3. Open the **Document** menu and choose **Insert Index Entry**, or press **⌘-Option-I**.
4. Text selected prior to the Insert Index Entry command will be enclosed by the characters *.i.* and *;* to denote the beginning and end of an index entry. (These characters are "hidden" and will not be printed.) If you have not specified text, the index entry symbols will surround the cursor. You can then type the index entry. Entries made in this manner will be "hidden." When you have finished, reposition the cursor on the page, and continue typing.
5. After using the Insert Index Entry command, select the **Preferences** command and choose **Show Hidden Text**. The index entry symbols and hidden entries will now be visible, allowing you to edit your entries prior to compiling the index.
6. To create multiple-level index entries, type a colon (:) between the main entry and subentries. Figure 22 provides an example of nested index entries, along with an illustration of how they will look in the final index.
7. To compile the index, select **Index** from the Utilities menu.

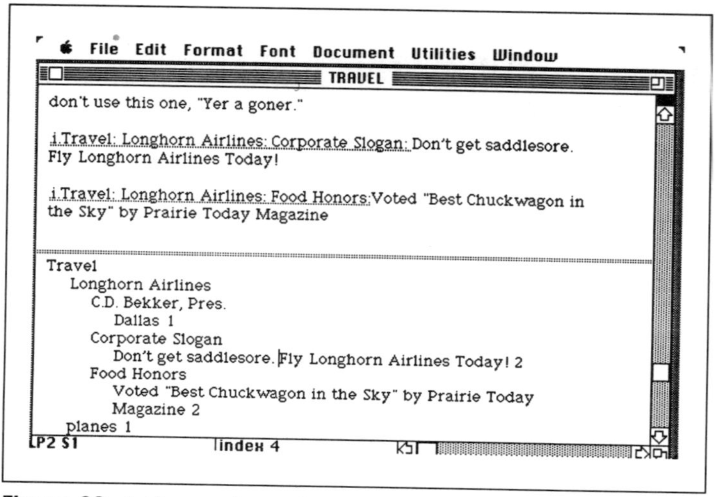

Figure 22: Index entries and compiled index

• NOTE It is advisable to create your entire document before inserting index entries. This allows you to more efficiently track the location and accuracy of the index entries spread throughout your document.

See Also *Index, Preferences*

INSERT PAGE BREAK

- **MENU** Document

- **DESCRIPTION** The Insert Page Break command allows you to manually select the location of page breaks in your documents.

To Insert a Page Break

1. Position the cursor at the location in your document where you want to have a page break inserted.
2. Open the **Document** menu and select **Insert Page Break**, or press **Shift-Enter**. The new page break will appear in your document.

INSERT TABLE

• **MENU** Document (Full Menus only)

• **DESCRIPTION** The Insert Tables command creates and formats text tables.

To Insert a Table

1. If not already selected, choose **Full Menus** from the Edit menu.
2. Move the cursor to the location in the document where you want the table to appear.
3. Open the **Document** menu.
4. Select **Insert Table**. The Insert Table dialog box will appear, as shown in Figure 23.

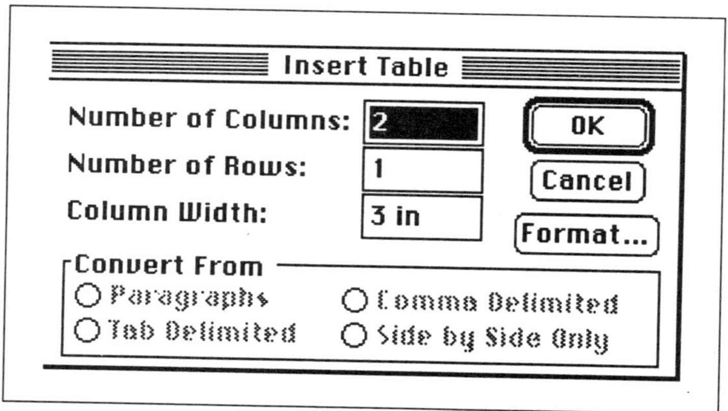

Figure 23: Insert Table dialog box

5. Define the format of the table using the following options:

Number of Columns: Specify the number of columns you want the table to include. You can change this number later by selecting **Table** from the Edit menu.

Number of Rows: Indicate the number of rows to be included in your table. This option is not available if the Comma Delimited option is selected in the Convert From box.

Column Width: Specifies the width of each column in your text table. Word automatically sets the distance between columns at .11 inch.

Convert From: Select **Paragraphs, Tab Delimited, Comma Delimited**, or **Side by Side Only** to indicate the format of the text being imported into your table.

> Select **Paragraph** for text documents you are inserting into a table format. Word will automatically reposition the text in the table to match carriage returns and page breaks in the original document.
>
> Select **Tab Delimited** to insert tab-delimited text into the table. A line which has been terminated with **Shift-Return** or **Shift-Enter** will be converted into a row of text.
>
> Select **Comma Delimited** when you are building a table from merged documents. Word treats Comma Delimited and Tab Delimited files exactly the same.
>
> Select **Side by Side Only** to convert side-by-side paragraphs created in Microsoft Word 3.0 into tables.

Format: Clicking on this button inserts your table and displays the Cells command dialog box so that you can reformat the table.

6. Click on **OK** or press **Return** to insert the table into your document.

See Also *Cells, Table*

INSERT TOC ENTRY

• **MENU** Document (Full Menus only)

• **DESCRIPTION** The Insert TOC Entry command marks words and phrases for inclusion in a table of contents.

To Insert a TOC Entry

1. If not already chosen, select **Full Menus** from the Edit menu.
2. Highlight the text to be included in the table of contents. If you have not entered the text you want to include in the table of contents, select **Insert TOC Entry** before typing the text. (Entries made in this manner will be "hidden" and will not print out with the text.)
3. Open the **Document** menu.
4. Select **Insert TOC Entry**.
5. The hidden text characters *.c.* and *.;.* will be inserted before the text to be indicate its inclusion in the table of contents. If you are typing the entry, reposition the cursor outside of the symbols once you have finished.
6. To view the hidden TOC characters, select **Show Hidden Text** from the **Preferences** command on the Edit menu. The TOC characters will appear in your document for your verification.

See Also *Paragraph, Preferences*

ITALICS

● **MENU** Format

● **DESCRIPTION** The Italics command toggles the italicization of text in your document.

To Italicize Text

1. Highlight the text you want italicized. If you do not specify text, subsequently typed text will be italicized.
2. Open the **Format** menu and select **Italic**, or press **⌘-Shift-I**.
3. The selected or subsequently typed text will appear italicized.
4. To turn off the italicization, select **Italic** again, or select **Plain Text** (**⌘-Shift-Z**).

See Also *Character*

NEW

• **MENU** File

• **DESCRIPTION** The New command creates a new document in Microsoft Word.

To Open a New Document

1. Open the **File** menu and select **New**, or press **⌘-N**.
2. A document window will appear. The cursor will be located in the upper left corner to indicate where text will appear when you begin typing.

• **NOTES** If the New command is dimmed on the File menu, save and close an open window.

You can also use the New command with the Spelling and Glossary commands. Choosing New while the Spelling dialog box is open creates a new dictionary, thus allowing you to create specialized dictionaries for your different Word documents. When used with the Glossary command, the New command creates a new glossary, clearing all glossary entries except for those included in the default Standard Glossary.

See Also *Save/Save As*

NEW WINDOW

• **MENU** Window (Full Menus only)

• **DESCRIPTION** The New Window command creates a second window for the current document, allowing you to view different parts of the same document at the same time.

To Open a Window

1. If not already selected, select **Full Menus** from the Edit menu.
2. Open the **Window** menu.
3. Select **New Window**.
4. A second copy of your document will now appear, in Galley View, in the foreground of your Macintosh screen. This window will be named *filename*:2 (where *filename* is the name of the document) to indicate that it is the second window of that document. You may open as many as 22 windows of the same document.
5. The names of the various open windows will appear on the Window menu. The active window will have visible scroll bars and a check mark (✓) next to its name on the Window menu. You may move between the various windows by opening the Window menu and selecting the desired window. You can also move to a window by clicking the mouse anywhere on that window.
6. To close a window, click on the small box in the upper left corner of that window.

OPEN

- **MENU** File

- **DESCRIPTION** The Open command accesses saved Word documents on your Macintosh hard disk or floppy diskette. The Open command can also open files which have been saved in selected other formats.

To Open a File

1. Open the File menu and select **Open**, or press **⌘-O**.
2. The **Open** dialog box will appear, with a list box from which you choose the document to open.
3. Search for the document using the list box scroll bar. You can change folders by clicking on the folder name above the list box. If you are searching a floppy disk, you can click on the **Eject** button to change disks. To search a different drive, click on the **Drive** button. (*Note:* If you have installed System 7 on your Macintosh, the **Drive** button will be labelled **Desktop**.)
4. Open the file you wish to modify by double-clicking on its name. You may also open the file by clicking on its name, and then clicking the **Open** button or pressing **Return**. If you wish only to view the file without making changes, click on the **Read Only** box prior to opening the file.

- **NOTES** The Open command will also open files in the Microsoft Works, MacWrite, MacPaint, and Microsoft RTF formats.

Press the Shift key when selecting Open to access any file on your disk. Documents in formats other than Word or the formats listed above will appear in ASCII (plain text) format.

You can use the Open command with the Define Styles, Glossary, and Spelling commands to open additional document style sheets, glossaries, and spell-checking dictionaries. When used with the Define Styles command, Open will merge the style sheet of the selected document with that of the current document.

See Also *Define Styles, Glossary, Save/Save As, Spelling, Styles*

OPEN HEADER/ OPEN FOOTER

• **MENU** Document

• **DESCRIPTION** You can use the Open Header and Open Footer commands to create, display, and revise headers (elements, such as section titles, that appear above the body of text on each page) and footers (elements that appear below the body of text).

To Create a Header or Footer

1. Open the **Documents** menu.
2. Select **Open Header** or **Open Footer**.
3. The header or footer window will appear. Type the desired header or footer in the window. Word also provides you with these preset entries:

   Page Number: Click on the page icon to automatically insert page numbers in the header or footer.

   Date: Click on the calendar icon to have the current date listed in the header or footer.

   Time: Click on the clock icon to include the time of day that you are printing the document.

   Same as Previous: Replaces the current header or footer with the previous header or footer in the document.

4. Click once on the small box in the upper left corner of the **Open Header** or **Open Footer** dialog box to return to your document.

See Also *Paragraph, Section*

OPEN MAIL

• **MENU** File (Full Menus only)

• **DESCRIPTION** The Open Mail command retrieves mail sent to you via Microsoft Mail. Microsoft Mail is a separate software package for sending mail between users on an Appletalk network. For more information on Appletalk networks, see Appendix A, *Using Microsoft Word on a Network.*

To Retrieve Mail

1. If not already selected, select **Full Menus** from the Edit menu.
2. Open the **File** menu.
3. Select **Open Mail**. The Open Mail dialog box will appear.
4. A list of messages sent to you via Microsoft Mail will appear in the list box.
5. Select the message to be viewed by double-clicking on its name with the mouse.
6. The message will appear in a new window, as shown in Figure 24. You can then save the message as a Word document by clicking on the **Save As** button, or you can **Forward**, **Delete**, **Reply** to, or **Copy** the message by clicking on the appropriate button. Clicking on the up or down arrow buttons will move you to the previous or next message, respectively.

See Also *Send Mail, Appendix A: Using Microsoft Word on a Network*

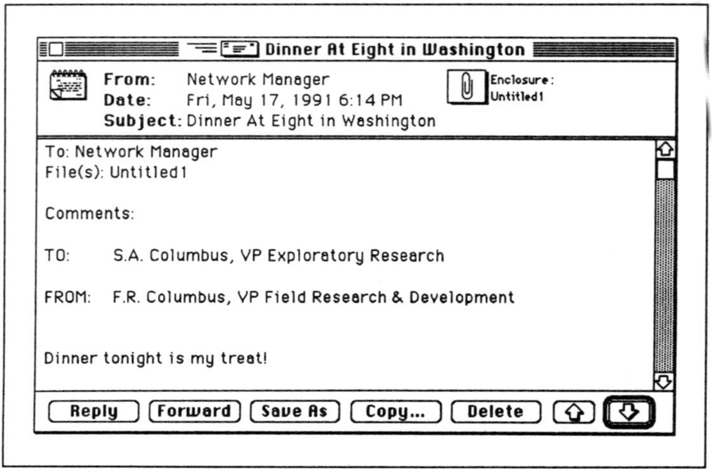

Figure 24: An open Microsoft Mail message

OUTLINE

• MENU Format

• DESCRIPTION The Outline command creates white, outlined characters.

To Create Outlined Characters

1. Select the text which you want to appear outlined. If you do not specify text, subsequently typed characters will appear outlined.
2. Open the **Format** menu.
3. Select **Outline**, or press **⌘-Shift-D**.
4. The text highlighted prior to the Outline command will now appear in outline format.
5. To terminate the outlining of characters, select **Outline** again, or select **Plain Text** (**⌘-Shift-Z**) from the Format menu.

See Also *Character*

OUTLINING

• **MENU** Document (Full Menus only)

• **DESCRIPTION** The Outlining command is a very useful tool for defining the hierarchical structure of your document. The Outlining command places your document in Outline View and displays the outline icon bar, which allows you to control the hierarchical placement of text.

To Create an Outline

1. If not already selected, select **Full Menus** from the Edit menu.
2. Open the **Document** menu.
3. Select **Outlining**. The Outline icon bar will appear along the top of the document window, and the document will be shown in Outline View, with headings positioned in hierarchical relation to one another.
4. If you are creating an outline, type the first outline heading at the cursor's location. A hollow minus sign will appear to the left of the text to indicate that the heading you are typing does not include any subordinate headings. Continue typing the other headings.
5. Click on the right arrow icon to subordinate a heading to a previous heading. The farther right a heading is moved, the more subordinate the heading is within the outline structure. The farther left a heading appears, the more significant it is within the outline's structure. When a heading is subordinated to another heading, the superior heading's minus sign will become a hollow plus sign.

6. You can use the icons on the Outline bar to modify the structure of your outline.

   ← Promote a heading.

   → Demote a heading.

   ↑ Move a heading up in the outline.

   ↓ Move a heading down in the outline.

   ⇒ Turn the heading into body text. Body text is text associated with a particular heading and is marked by a hollow box.

   ▤ Hide or show the body text of your document.

   ff View the document's formatting structure.

   ▤ Show all outlining levels.

   Click on the plus sign icon to display or the minus sign icon to hide the subordinate headings and text for a selected heading. You can also display subordinate headings and text by double-clicking on a heading's hollow plus sign icon.

   You can specify the number of outline levels Word will display by clicking on 1, 2, 3, or 4 on the Outline icon bar. Clicking on 1 will display only level one headings.

7. Select **Outlining** from the Document Menu, or press **⌘-U**, to switch back to the Galley View of your document.

• **EXAMPLE** Longhorn Airlines is planning to begin direct service to Arizona, California, and Nevada from Dallas, Houston, and Austin. An outline of the marketing plan for the expanded routes has been created (Figure 25). Note that the document in Figure 25 is already in Outline View and the Outline bar is displayed along the top of the Window.

The Marketing Director for Longhorn reviewed the outline and decided to add an Executive Summary and a Promotions section.

1. Place the cursor in front of the "Marketing Plan" heading, type **Executive Summary**, and press **Return**. "Executive

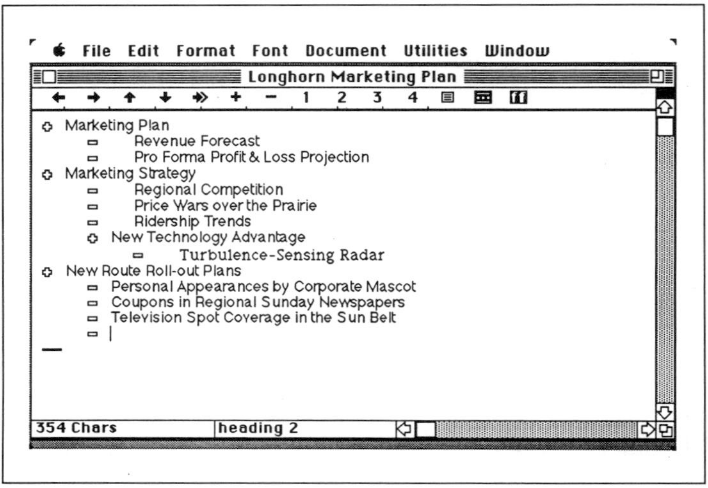

Figure 25: Longhorn Airlines' marketing plan outline

Summary" will now be a level one heading. The "Marketing Plan" entry will be subordinated to "Executive Summary."

2. Click on the left arrow to promote "Marketing Plan" to the first heading level.
3. To add the "Promotions" section, place the cursor at the leftmost location of the Outline View window directly below the "Television Spot Coverage in Sun Belt" heading.
4. Type **Promotions**.
5. "Promotions" is now a level one heading.
6. Longhorn Airlines' Marketing Director has also decided to move the "Pro Forma Profit & Loss Projection" in the Marketing Plan to the Executive Summary. To do this, use the Cut and Paste commands to move the "Profit & Loss Projection" from the Marketing Plan section to the Executive Summary.
7. The outline should now look like Figure 26.

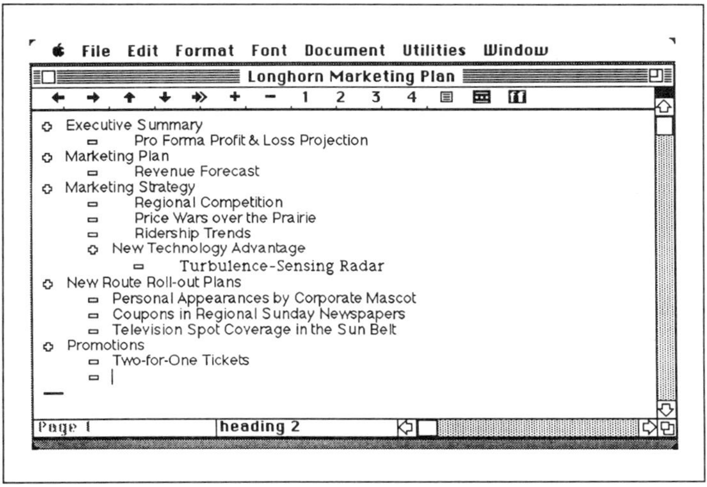

Figure 26: Outline after revision

PAGE SETUP

• **MENU** File

• **DESCRIPTION** The Page Setup command defines paper size, print orientation, and whatever printer effects you want applied to your documents.

To Set Printer Options

1. Open the **File** menu.
2. Select **Page Setup**, or press **Shift-F8** using the function key located on the Apple keyboard.
3. The Page Setup dialog box will appear, presenting you with a series of options outlined in the Options section below. The listed options will vary depending on the type of printer selected in the Chooser box. Compare Figures 27 and 28.
4. Use the options in the Page Setup dialog box to define your document's printed appearance.
5. Click on **OK** to apply the selected options.

Options

The following options are available for all printers:

Paper: Selects the type of paper you plan to use in your printer. If you are printing on an ImageWriter, you may choose between US Letter, US Legal, A4 Letter, International Fanfold, and Computer paper. If you are using a LaserWriter, your choices are US Letter, US Legal, A4 Letter, Tabloid, and B5 Letter.

Orientation: Determines if your document will be printed with lines across the width or along the length of the page. The vertical and horizontal images of a human figure illustrate how the printer will print your document. Choosing the standing

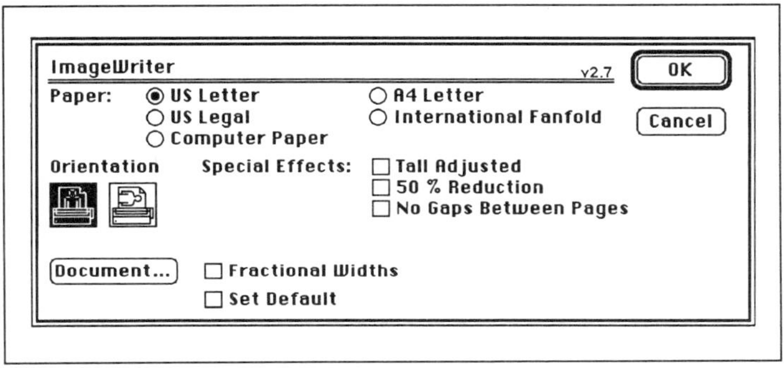

Figure 27: Page Setup dialog box for the Apple ImageWriter

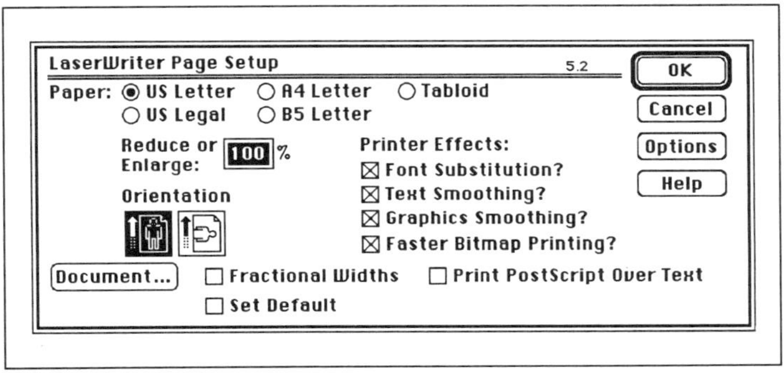

Figure 28: Page Setup dialog box for the Apple LaserWriter

human figure ( ) renders your document in "portrait" orientation, the most common print orientation. Selecting the horizontal image ( ) will print your document in "landscape" orientation, with print lines running along the length of the page.

Document: Opens the Document command dialog box. Select this if you need to redefine the parameters of your document to match the specifications of the selected printer. After you have reset the document's parameters, click on **OK** to apply or

Cancel to discard your modifications. The Page Setup dialog box will reappear.

The following options are specific to the Apple LaserWriter:

Reduce or Enlarge: Prints the document at the relative size indicated in the option reference box. The default value for this option is 100%.

Font Substitution: Replaces non-LaserWriter fonts with LaserWriter fonts. For example, this option substitutes Times font for New York, Helvetica font for Geneva, and Courier font for Monaco.

Text Smoothing: Prints extra-high quality text at the cost of slowing print time.

Graphics Smoothing: Prints extra-high quality, smooth-edged graphics at the cost of slowing print time.

Faster Bitmap Printing: Selects a lower-resolution imaging mode for faster printing.

Fractional Widths: This option spaces fonts to a fraction of a point. This creates better spaced characters and words in some fonts but might make the screen display of the text appear ragged. (*Note:* If this option does not work properly, deinstall your fonts with Apple's Font/DA Mover, and reinstall them with version 3.6 of the Font/DA Mover.)

Print PostScript Over Text: Select this option to print an imported PostScript graphic file over existing text. This option can be useful for placing text labels and pointers in graphic images.

Set Default: Saves the current selections as the new default values.

• **NOTES** Whenever a new printer is selected in the Chooser dialog box, use the Page Setup command to reset the page parameters for all open documents. This will ensure that your printed pages appear as you intend.

The Page Setup command assumes that you will be using the same printer throughout your Word session. Changes made in the Page Setup dialog box for a specific document will remain in effect until you change the Page Setup parameters, choose another printer, or end your session.

The available print options in the Page Setup dialog box vary depending on the model of printer selected in the Chooser box. Options other than those listed here may also appear. See your printer manual for further information regarding the print options available for your printer.

See Also *Chooser, Document, Page View, Paragraph, Print, Print Preview*

PAGE VIEW

• **MENU** Document

• **DESCRIPTION** The Page View command switches between the Galley and Page Views of your document. On startup, Word uses Galley View, which displays text in a single column and hides headers, footers, and page numbers. Page View displays the page with all its formatting but slows down editing speed. You can edit text while in Page View.

To Toggle the Page View Mode

1. Open the **Document** menu.
2. Select **Page View**, or press **⌘-B**.
3. The active window will now be in Page View, showing how your document will look when it is printed.
4. A check mark (✓) will appear next to the Page View command in the Document menu, indicating that the Page View mode is active.
5. Select **Page View** again to return to the Galley View of your document.

See Also *Preferences, Print Preview*

PARAGRAPH

• MENU Format (Full Menus only)

• DESCRIPTION Use the Paragraph command to format paragraphs. You can select indentation points, line spacing, tab locations, paragraph borders, page breaks and text justification in your document.

To Format Paragraphs

1. If not already selected, select **Full Menus** from the Edit Menu.
2. Open the **Format** menu.
3. Select **Paragraph**, or press **⌘-M**. Alternatively, you can double-click on the right indent marker (◀) on the ruler to access the Paragraph dialog box.
4. The Paragraph dialog box will appear as shown in Figure 29. You can also access the **Tabs**, **Borders** and **Position** dialog boxes by clicking on the relevant buttons.

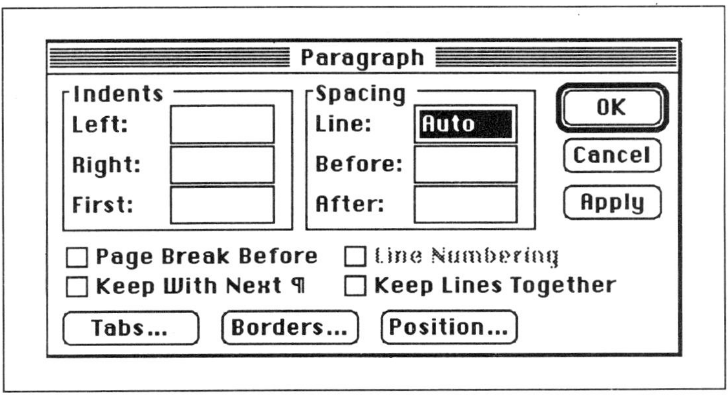

Figure 29: Paragraph dialog box

5. Format your paragraphs using the options listed below.
6. When you have made your formatting selections, click on **OK** or press **Return**. The options selected in the Paragraph dialog box will be applied to your document.

OPTIONS

Indents: This option sets the horizontal distance of the paragraph from the left margin. You can specify this distance in inches (*in*), centimeters (*cm*), points (*pt*), or picas (*pi*). Word assumes that you are specifying the distance in point size. (One point equals approximately 1/72 inch.) The **Left, Right,** and **First** options set the indent from the left and right margins and for the first paragraph line, respectively.

Spacing: The three boxes in this portion of the Paragraph dialog box designate the amount of space between successive lines of text in your paragraphs. The units of measure used with Indents also apply to these settings.

The Line spacing default value is "Auto." You can specify either **Auto** or **0** for single spacing. If you prefer a different spacing for your document, type the value in the Line box. Be sure to specify the unit of measure.

Use the **Before** and **After** boxes to specify the amount of space to insert at the beginning and end of paragraphs.

Page Break Before: This option inserts a page break immediately before the paragraph being formatted.

Keep With Next ¶: This option automatically joins the selected paragraph with the following paragraph. Use this option to keep closely related paragraphs, such as figures with captions, together on the same page.

Line Numbering: Select this option to add line numbers to your document. These numbers will only be displayed when you are in Page View. You must select the Line Number option in the Section command located on the Format menu in order to select this option.

Keep Lines Together: This option prevents a paragraph from being split by a page break. Use this option when the entire paragraph must appear on the same page.

Tabs: You may set the Tabs by clicking on the **Tabs** button. The Tabs dialog box will appear, as shown in Figure 30.

Center: Centers text on the tab stop.

Left: Aligns text to the right of the tab stop.

Right: Aligns text to the left of the tab stop.

Decimal: Automatically aligns any decimal points in the text on the tab location.

Bar: Places a vertical bar at the designated location. This is not a tab stop and is not accessible with the tab key.

Leader: Specifies the type of leader, if any, to be placed between the text at the tab stop and any preceding text: ellipse (…), dashed line, or solid line.

Set: Sets the tab stops listed in the dialog box.

Clear: Clears the selected tab stop.

Clear All: Clears all tab stops and resets tabs to the Document command default values.

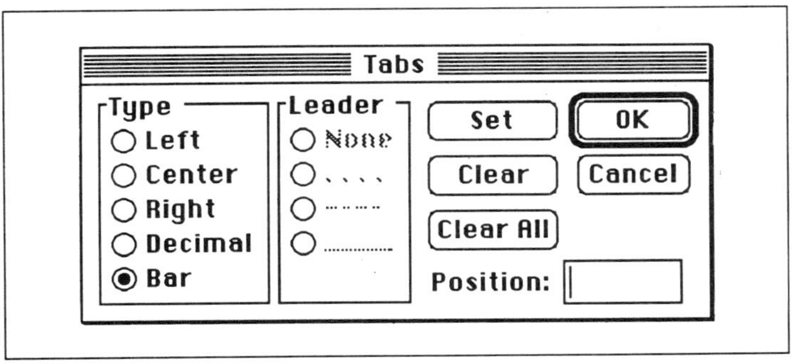

Figure 30: Tabs dialog box

Position: Sets a tab stop in a specific location, such as 2.75 inches, from the left margin.

Borders: Opens the Paragraph Borders dialog box which allows you to place borders around your paragraphs. For a full description of this option, see the *Borders* command reference.

Position: Allows you to place the paragraph anywhere on the printable portion of a page. For a complete description of this option, see the *Position* command reference.

See Also *Borders, Document, Position, Preferences, Section, Show Ruler/Hide Ruler*

PASTE

- **MENU** Edit

- **DESCRIPTION** The Paste command moves images and text from the Clipboard to your documents.

To Insert Text or Graphics

1. Move the cursor to the place in your document where you want the text or graphic image pasted.
2. Open the **Edit** menu and select **Paste**, or press **⌘-V**.
3. The contents of the Clipboard will be pasted directly into your document.

See Also *Copy, Cut, Paste Link, Save/Save As*

PASTE LINK

- **Menu** Edit (Full Menus only)

- **DESCRIPTION** The Paste Link command links specific information from other Macintosh applications into your Microsoft Word documents. This is particularly useful for including information that changes on a periodic basis, such as a monthly totals from a spreadsheet.

To Create a Link

1. Set your Macintosh to run under MultiFinder. You can do this by selecting Set Startup from the Special menu on the system desktop and restarting the machine.
2. Once MultiFinder is active on your system, select the application from which you want to paste information into your Word document.
3. Select the information or range to be copied into your Microsoft Word document.
4. Open the **Edit** menu and select **Copy**, or press **⌘-C**, to copy the selected text onto the Clipboard.
5. Using MultiFinder, switch to Microsoft Word.
6. Open the Word document that will receive the linked information and position the cursor at the desired insertion point.
7. Open the **Edit** menu, and select **Paste Link**.
8. The information saved to the Clipboard will now be pasted into your document at the cursor's location.

- **NOTES** QuickSwitch is the name of the Microsoft Word utility that supports the Paste Link, Edit Link, and Update Link commands. QuickSwitch inserts hidden identifiers into the Word document to indicate the information's host application and file. The syntax for this identifier is *Application!filename* where the exclamation point (!) is a delimiter. For Microsoft Excel spreadsheets, the syntax is *Application!filename!areaname* where *areaname* is a specific spreadsheet range.

You can create a link manually by typing in the identifier and formatting it as hidden text with the Character command. For applications which are not supported by QuickSwitch, you must use a utility like Fedit or ResEdit to find the application's four-letter "name."

See Also *Edit Link, Update Link*

PLAIN FOR STYLE

• **MENU** Format

• **DESCRIPTION** The Plain for Style command resets enhanced text to its basic format. If text has been bolded, italicized, or resized, the Plain for Style command will revert the style of selected text to the default style of the paragraph.

To Reset Text to Default Formatting

1. Select the text to be reset to default formatting.
2. Open the **Format** menu.
3. Select **Plain for Style**, or press **⌘-Shift-Spacebar**.
4. The text will now appear in the default style of the paragraph.

See Also *Character, Define Styles, Plain Text, Styles, Undo/Redo*

PLAIN TEXT

• MENU Format

• DESCRIPTION The Plain Text command to resets the character style of selected text, without changing character spacing, font, font size, or super- and subscripts.

To Restore Plain Text

1. Select the text to be changed.
2. Open the **Format** menu.
3. Select **Plain Text**, or press **⌘-Shift-Z**.
4. The highlighted text will retain its font, size, spacing and position but lose any other attributes (such as boldfacing or italicization).

• NOTE You can use Plain Text to turn off any currently active Bold, Italic, Outline, Shadow, or Underline commands.

See Also *Character, Define Styles, Plain for Styles, Styles, Undo/Redo*

POSITION

- **MENU** Format (Full Menus only)

- **DESCRIPTION** The Position command lets you control the placement of any text block or graphic image on the printable portion of a page. You can use Word commands to add borders or other enhancements to the positioned object.

To Position a Text Block or Graphic Image

1. If not already selected, select **Full Menus** from the Edit Menu.
2. Select the block or object to be positioned.
3. Open the **Format** menu.
4. Select **Position**. The Position dialog box will appear, as shown in Figure 31.

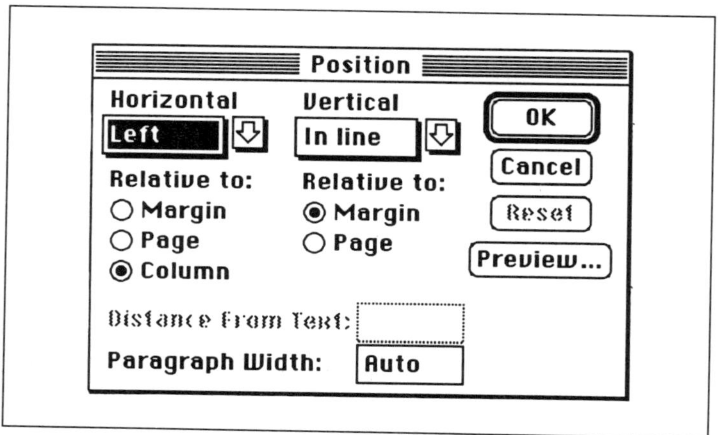

Figure 31: Position dialog box

5. Position the object using the options listed below.
6. Select **Preview** from the Position dialog box. The new position of the object will be displayed on screen.
7. When you are satisfied with the positioning of the object, click on the **OK** button, or press **Return**.

OPTIONS

Horizontal: Controls the left-to-right positioning of the text block or graphic image. Use the pop-up menu to place the object along the **Left** boundary, **Right** boundary, or **Centered** between boundaries. The **Inside** option positions the text or graphics on the right boundary for even-numbered pages and on the left boundary for odd-numbered pages. The **Outside** option positions the object on the left boundary for even-numbered pages and on the right boundary for odd-numbered pages. Typing a measurement into the "Horizontal" box will position the object the specified distance from the left boundary.

Relative to: Sets the boundary used to establish horizontal positioning. You can select from among **Margin, Page,** and **Column**.

Vertical: Controls the top-to-bottom positioning of the text block or graphic image. Select **In line, Top, Center**, or **Bottom** to designate the position of your selected item on the page. **In line** places the object in the first available free area on the page. If you type a measurement in the "Vertical" box, the object will be positioned that distance from the top boundary.

Relative to: Set the boundary used to establish vertical position. You can select from either the **Margin** or the edge of the **Page**.

Distance From Text: Sets the amount of space between the object and surrounding text on the page. Enter the amount of space in points to define the distance. (One point equals approximately 1/72 inch.)

Paragraph Width: Sets the width of the selected paragraph or text block in your document. **Auto** sets the width to that of the text column.

Reset: Returns the selected object to its original position.

Preview: Saves the settings in the Position dialog box, closes the Position dialog box, and displays the Print Preview perspective of your document. All Print Preview options are now available for use in modifying the document.

OK: Applies the selections made and closes the dialog box.

Cancel: Cancels the options you have selected and closes the dialog box.

• **NOTE** You can see the actual location of positioned objects by selecting Page View or Print Preview. Word will not display the objects in their specified location while in Galley View.

See Also *Define Styles, Page View, Paragraph, Preferences, Print Preview*

PREFERENCES

• MENU Edit (Full Menus only)

• DESCRIPTION The Preferences command lets you configure Word to your specifications. You can set the default units of measure, show hidden text, insert gridlines, display documents in Page View, enable background repagination and "smart" quotes, and define how Word will manage your system's memory.

To Select Viewing Options

1. If not already selected, select **Full Menus** from the Edit menu.
2. Open the **Edit** menu.
3. Select **Preferences**.
4. The Preferences dialog box will appear, as shown in Figure 32.
5. Select the desired viewing options. These are outlined in the Options section below.
6. After selecting the desired options, click on **OK**, or press **Return**.
7. The options selected in the Preferences dialog box will be reflected in the current and subsequent Word sessions.

OPTIONS

Default Measure: Sets the default unit of measure for all Word commands. Measurements may be listed in inches, centimeters, points, or picas. (One point equals approximately 1/72 inch; one pica equals approximately 1/6 inch.) Expanded and condensed text, super- and subscripts, and line spacing will continue to use points as the unit of measure.

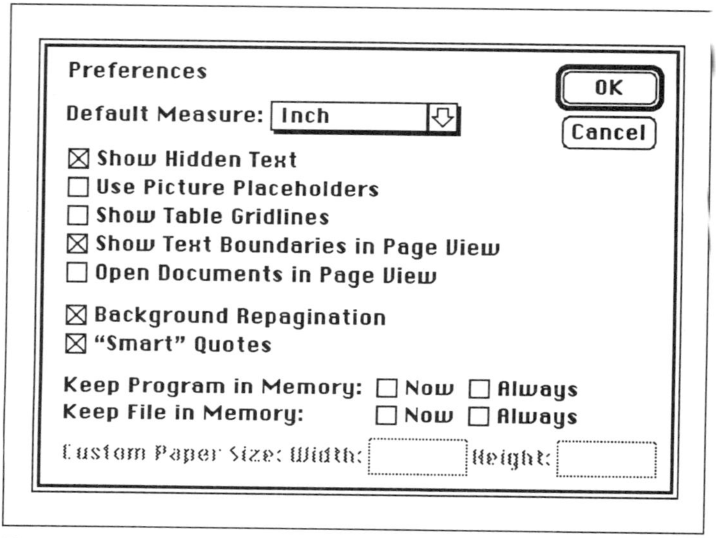

Figure 32: Preferences dialog box

Show Hidden Text: Selecting this option will display text and characters that have been embedded in your document. To print out hidden text, select the **Print Hidden Text** option from the Print dialog box.

Use Picture Placeholders: Substitutes gray rectangles for graphics in the text display in order to speed scrolling and screen displays.

Show Table Gridlines: Shows the gridlines between the rows and columns in tables. These gridlines will not be printed.

Show Text Boundaries in Page View: This option is useful for positioning text and graphic elements on pages with overlapping text blocks.

Background Repagination: This option paginates your documents automatically whenever you are not typing. It may slow text entry in large documents.

"Smart" Quotes: Instructs Word to print typeset-quality quotation marks instead of standard keyboard quotation marks.

Keep Program In Memory: When Word is first launched from the Macintosh desktop, the main program files are loaded into the computer's memory. This option loads as many of the program files from the hard disk into your system's memory as possible, thereby speeding overall program execution. Select **Now** to maximize the number of program files in the memory for the current editing session only. Select **Always** to maximize the number of program files loaded into the memory for future Word sessions.

Keep File in Memory: Maximizes the number of document files loaded into the Macintosh's available memory. Select **Now** to load the files into memory during the current Word session. Select **Always** to load the maximum number of document files into the memory at the start of future Word sessions.

Custom Paper Size: When you have selected either the Apple ImageWriter or ImageWriter LQ from the Chooser dialog box, the Custom Paper Size option will be visible in the Preferences dialog box. Use this option to set the paper size used in printing documents.

See Also *Hide ¶/Show ¶, Insert Index Entry, Insert Table, Insert TOC Entry, Repaginate Now*

PRINT

• **MENU** File

• **DESCRIPTION** The Print command prints open documents. The options available in the Print dialog box are determined by the printer selected in the Chooser option in the Apple menu. For a more detailed description of how the Chooser printer selection affects printing, see *Page Setup*.

To Print a Document

1. Open the **File** menu and select **Print**, or press **⌘-P**.
2. The Print dialog box will appear. The number of options listed in the box depends on your model of printer. Figure 33 shows the print options for the Apple ImageWriter while Figure 34 shows the options for the LaserWriter. Select the desired print options, described in the Options section below.
3. Click on **OK**, or press **Return**. Your document will begin printing.

Options

Copies: Selects the number of copies to be printed. At the end of each print session, this number reverts to one, regardless of the number of copies requested in previous print sessions.

Pages *(LaserWriter)*/**Page Range** *(ImageWriter)*: Select **All** to print the entire document. If you want to print only a section of your document, specify the starting and ending page numbers in the **From** and **To** boxes.

Paper Source: Indicates the type of paper to be used in printing your document. Selecting the **Automatic** button for the ImageWriter or **Paper Cassette** for the LaserWriter will continue to feed sheets to the printer until the entire document has

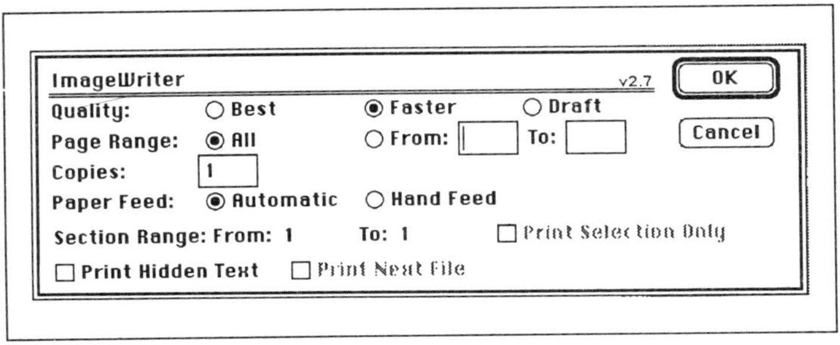

Figure 33: Print dialog box: ImageWriter

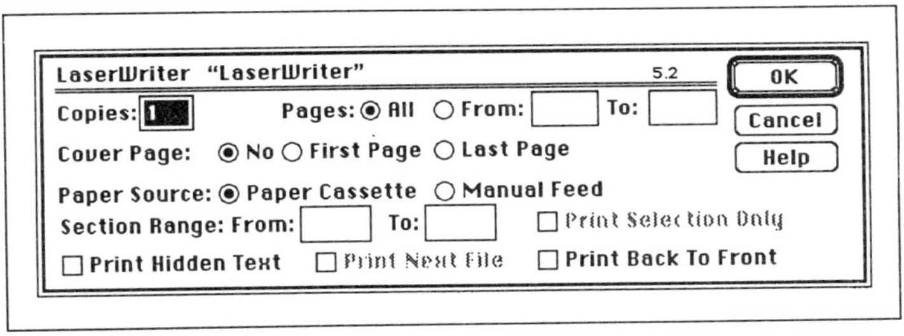

Figure 34: Print dialog box: LaserWriter

been printed. Selecting **Hand Feed** for the ImageWriter or **Manual Feed** for the LaserWriter will tell Word to pause after each page so that you may load another sheet of paper. Select **Continue** to continue printing.

Section Range: Indicates which sections, as defined by the Section command, you wish to print.

Print Selection Only: Select this option to print only selected text in your document.

Print Hidden Text: Prints hidden text and codes, such as Table of Contents entry codes, index entry codes, PostScript codes, and QuickSwitch text.

Print Next File: Prints the Next File specified in the Document dialog box.

If you are using an ImageWriter or compatible printer, you may select the following option:

Quality: For the highest print quality (at a loss of print speed), select **Best**. Select **Faster** to print your document with average quality and speed. The **Draft** selection will print the document at the fastest rate but will ignore character styles (such as italics, bold, and outline styles) and paragraph formatting.

If you are using a LaserWriter or compatible printer, you may also choose the following options:

Cover Page: Indicates whether you want to print a cover page listing the date, time, and LaserWriter identification at the beginning of the document, the end of the document, or not at all.

Print Back to Front: Select this option to print your document in backwards sequential page order, *i.e.*, from last page to first page. This option is only available for printers that print pages exiting the printer text face up.

● **NOTE** The Print command can also be used to print style sheets (when the Define Styles dialog box is open), glossaries (when the Glossary dialog box is open), outlines (if Outlining is on), and selected text.

See Also *Chooser, Define Styles, Document, Glossary, Outlining, Page Setup, Page View, Print Preview*

PRINT MERGE

• MENU File

• DESCRIPTION The Print Merge command combines the text of a main document and the information of a data document to print a series of form letters. The main document includes the letter or text that will not change. The data document contains the information that changes in each document, such as addresses and salutations.

To Create a Form Letter

1. Create the standard letter or document. Indicate the location in your document where merged data is to be inserted by typing «*fieldname*», where *fieldname* is the name of a data field in the corresponding data document. The guillemets («») are entered by pressing **Option-** for « and **Option-Shift-** for ».

   n the first line of your main document, type **«DATA *data document*»**, where *data document* is the name of the data document file.

2. Next, create your data document. The contents of your data document will specify the information that is specific to each version of the final document. The codes to be used in creating the data document are explained in the Option section of this command reference. The first line of the data document must be the field names, separated by commas or tab marks. Type the data records on succeeding lines in the same order as the field name line, with fields separated by commas or tab marks.

3. After creating the main and data documents, place them both in the same folder.

4. Open the main document.

5. Open the **File** menu and select the **Print Merge**. The Print Merge dialog box will appear.

6. Specify the records in the data document that you want merged and printed. You can merge all records by clicking on the **All** button or merge selected records by specifying a range in the **From** and **To** boxes. (The first line following the field name line in the data document is record one.)

7. Click on the **Print** button to display the Print dialog box and begin the printing of merged documents. Alternatively, you can click on **New Document** to create a new document file for the merged file, which can then be edited and printed normally.

8. To return to the main document without performing a print merge, click on **Cancel**.

Field Options for Main and Data Documents

«ASK *field* = ?»: Automatically prompts the user for the text to be inserted in the document.

«ASK *field* = ?*prompt*»: Uses the *prompt* text to ask the user for input.

«DATA *data file name*»: Specifies the data document name you want to use in completing the Print Merge command. This *must* be the first line of the main document.

«IF *field=data*»*text*...«ENDIF»: Merges *text* into the main document if the listed condition *field* = *data* is met. You may use the following logical operators to specify the condition:

=	Exactly matches the specified text.
>	Searches for a larger text string than the specified text.
<	Searches for a text string of fewer characters than the specified string.
>=	Searches for a text string greater than or equal to the specified text string.
<=	Searches for text that is less than or equal to the specified text string.
<>	Searches for a string which does not match the specified string.

«IF *field=data*»*text*...«ELSE»*text*...«ENDIF»: This is the same as the **«IF»...«ENDIF»** command, with the added function that if the condition *field=data* is not met, then the text after «ELSE» is used.

«INCLUDE *document*»: Inserts text from the named document directly into the main document.

«NEXT»: Moves the merge to the next data record. This is useful for printing mailing labels or other times when you want to print many data records on a single page.

«SET *field=data*»: Instructs Word to insert the specified *data* into the indicated *field*. Data set in this command will not vary from copy to copy; it will stay constant.

«SET *field=?*»: Instructs Word to prompt the user for input during the merge of the first record. The entered data will then be included in each subsequent document in the merge.

«SET *field =?prompt*»: This is the same as «SET *field* = ?» except that it uses the *prompt* text to ask the user for input.

See Also *Chooser, Page Setup, Preferences, Print*

PRINT PREVIEW

• **MENU** File

• **DESCRIPTION** The Print Preview command lets you view your document's appearance on a page prior to its printing. Icons located in the Print Preview screen can be used to modify the location of page numbers, margins and page breaks in your document.

To Preview a Document

1. Open the **File** menu.
2. Select **Print Preview**, or press **⌘-I**.
3. The Print Preview view of your document will appear.
4. Use the icons to modify the view of you document.

   Page Number Icon: Click and drag this icon to place a page number anywhere on the page. Double-clicking on the icon will position the page number in the upper right corner of the page, or in the upper-left corner of even-numbered pages if the Mirror option is selected.

   Margin Icon: Clicking on this icon shows the margins, page breaks, and boundaries within your documents. Click on and drag the margin, boundary, or page break to change its location.

5. You can move directly to the Print command dialog box by clicking on the printer icon. You can also move directly to the Page View of your document by clicking on **Page View**.
6. To exit Print Preview, click on **Cancel**.

See Also *Page Setup, Page View, Paragraph, Position, Print*

QUIT

- **MENU** File

- **DESCRIPTION** The Quit command ends your Word session. If you have made changes to an open file but have not saved them prior to issuing the Quit command, Word will ask if you want to save the changes and will open the Save As dialog box.

To End Your Word Session

1. Open the **File** menu and select **Quit**, or press **⌘-Q**.
2. If you have not made any changes to your document since the last Save command, Word will just quit and return you to the Macintosh desktop. Otherwise, Word will ask you if you want to save the changes in the document. Click on **Yes** to save the changes or **No** to exit without change. If you opt to save the changes in an untitled document, Word will open the Save As dialog box and ask you to enter a name for the new document.
3. To return to Word, click on **Cancel**.

See Also *Save/Save As*

RENUMBER

- **MENU** Utilities (Full Menus only)

- **DESCRIPTION** The Renumber command numbers (or renumbers) selected paragraphs in your document. You can use Arabic numerals, Roman numerals, or upper and lowercase letters to designate the successive paragraphs.

To Number Paragraphs

1. If not already selected, select **Full Menus** from the Edit menu.
2. If you wish to number a specific series of paragraphs, use the mouse to highlight the paragraphs.
3. Open the **Utilities** menu and select **Renumber**. The Renumber dialog box will appear.
4. Use the options below to define the scope and type of numbering:

   Paragraphs: Select **All** to number every paragraph in your selection. If you have not highlighted any paragraphs, then every paragraph in the document will be numbered. Lines ending with a paragraph symbol (¶) but not containing any text will not be numbered. Select **Only If Already Numbered** to number only those paragraphs that have previously been numbered.

   Start At: Specifies the starting number. The default is one. If the paragraphs have already been numbered, the box will display the number of the first numbered paragraph of the selection.

Format: Indicates the format for paragraph numbers, using the symbols below (Arabic numerals and period separators are the default).

Symbol	Type
Numbering Formats	
1	Arabic numerals (1,2,3…)
I	Uppercase Roman numerals (I, II, III…)
A	Uppercase letters (A, B, C…)
i	Lowercase Roman numerals (i, ii, iii…)
a	Lowercase letters (a, b, c…)
Separator Characters	
.	period
,	comma
-	hyphen
/	slash
:	colon
()	left or right parenthesis
[]	left or right bracket
{}	left or right brace

Numbers: Defines the numbering style for each paragraph level. Paragraph levels are defined by the Outlining command or indentation relative to the left margin. Clicking the **1** button numbers each paragraph with a single whole number, regardless of the paragraph's level. Selecting **1.1** numbers the paragraphs according to level, as shown below:

1

1.1

1.2

1.2.1

By Example sets the numbering scheme to that of the first paragraph of each level in the document. **Remove** discards all numbers from the selection.

5. Click on **OK** to apply your selections to the document.

REPAGINATE NOW

• **MENU** Document (Full Menus only)

• **DESCRIPTION** The Repaginate Now command manually paginates (sets page breaks in) your documents.

To Automatically Set Page Breaks

1. If not already selected, choose **Full Menus** from the Edit menu.
2. Select the **Preferences** command from the Edit menu and make sure that the Show Hidden Text option is turned off. Otherwise, hidden text will be included in the Repaginate Now command's page length calculations.
3. Open the **Document** menu and select **Repaginate Now**, or press ⌘ **-J**.
4. Word will automatically place new page breaks in your document.

• **NOTES** If background repagination is selected in the Preferences dialog box, Word repaginates your document whenever the keyboard is idle. You can still use the Repaginate Now command to make sure that the document's pagination is up-to-date. The background repagination will remain in effect.

The Repaginate Now command does not recalculate the size and spacing of unchanged paragraphs. If the repagination produces unsatisfactory results, you can recalculate the size of all page elements (including unedited paragraphs) by holding down the Shift key when selecting Repaginate Now.

See Also *Galley View, Page View, Preferences, Print Preview*

SAVE/SAVE AS

• MENU File

• DESCRIPTION The Save and Save As commands save your document to a file on hard or floppy disk.

To Save a Document

1. After creating or editing your document, open the **File** menu and select **Save**, or press **⌘-S**. If you wish to save your document under a new name, select **Save As** from the File menu, or press **Shift-F7**.
2. If you have already saved your document, Word will save any changes under the same document name. If you have not previously saved the document, or if you selected the Save As command, the Save As dialog box will appear, as shown in Figure 35.
3. The list box located in the upper left corner of the Save As dialog box shows the names of files already saved in the

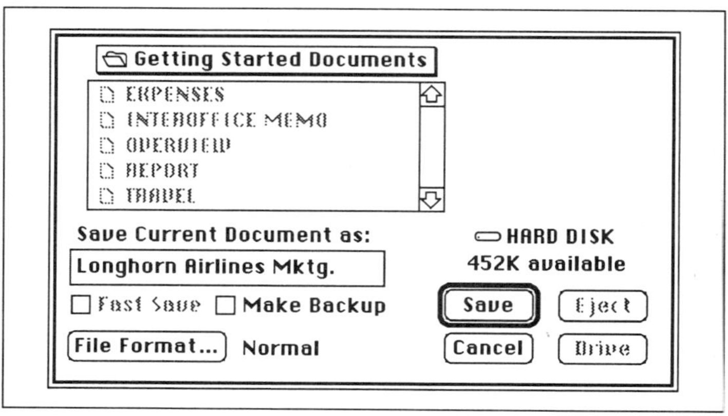

Figure 35: The Save As dialog box

current folder. Enter a name for the document in the **Save Current Document as** box. If you wish to replace the contents of an existing document, enter the document's name in the box.

4. You can change folders by clicking on the folder name above the list box and, while holding down the mouse button, dragging the mouse pointer to the desired folder name.

5. To switch between the hard or floppy drives, click on the **Drive** button. To change floppy disks, click on the **Eject** button.

6. You can select **Fast Save** to speed the process of saving files. Fast Save will store more of your document in the system's memory, writing only modifications directly to disk. This will make file saving faster but will also increase the size of your document files. You cannot use the Fast Save and Make Backup options together.

7. You can select **Make Backup** to have a second copy of the document, named "Backup of *document*," saved to the same location as the original document. Selecting Make Backup will gray out Fast Save, making it unavailable for selection.

8. To save the document, click on the **Save** button, or press **Return**. If you are replacing the contents of an existing document file, click on **Replace** when Word asks for confirmation of the action. You can now quit from Word, if you wish, by pressing **⌘-Q**.

To Save a Document to Another Format

1. If not already selected, select **Full Menus** from the Edit menu.

2. After creating or editing your document, open the **File** menu and select **Save As**, or press **Shift-F7**.

3. Specify the document name, folder, and drive as outlined above in Steps 3–5 of the "To Save a Document" section.

4. Click on the **File Format** button. The File Format options box will appear, as shown in Figure 36.

5. Select the desired format in which the file will be saved.

Normal: Saves the document in Microsoft Word 4.0 format.

Text Only: Saves the document as a standard ASCII (plain text) file. Paragraph marks, end-of-line marks, section marks and page break marks are converted to ASCII return characters. Other formatting is lost.

Text Only With Line Breaks: Similar to the Text Only format but adds ASCII return characters after each line in order to eliminate long, unbroken lines of text. Use this option if you plan to send the saved document via modem to another location.

Microsoft Word 1.0/Microsoft Works: Saves the file in a format readable by version 1.0 of Microsoft Word and Microsoft Works version 1.0. If you wish to use the saved file in Microsoft Works 2.0 or higher, use the Rich Text Format (RTF) option. Certain features, such as tables, color designations, and absolute tab positions, may be lost.

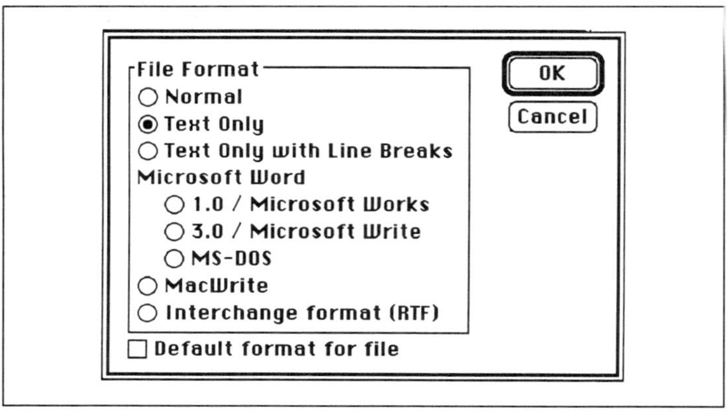

Figure 36: File Format options box.

Microsoft Word 3.0/Microsoft Write: Saves your document in a format for use with version 3.0 of Microsoft Word or with Microsoft Write. Certain features, such as tables, color designations, and absolute tab positions, may be lost.

MS-DOS: Saves your document for later use with Microsoft Word 4.0 on the IBM PC and compatibles. If you wish to use the document in Microsoft Word 5.0 or later on the IBM PC, use the Rich Text Format (RTF) option. Certain features, such as tables, color designations, and absolute tab positions, may be lost, but character and paragraph formatting will be saved.

MacWrite: Saves the file for use in MacWrite (from Claris). Certain features, such as tables, color designations, and absolute tab positions, may be lost.

Interchange Format: Saves your document in Microsoft's Rich Text Format (RTF). This format uses special ASCII codes to preserve document formatting for use in other Microsoft and third-party programs that read this format.

To make the new format the default for the *current* document and Word session, click in the **Default format for file** box.

6. Click on the **OK** button to return to the Save As dialog box, or click on **Cancel** to keep the previous file format. The new format will be displayed next to the File Format button.
7. Save your document as outlined in the previous section.

See Also *Commands, Full Menus/Short Menus, Preferences.*

SECTION

• **MENU** Format (Full Menus only)

• **DESCRIPTION** Used to define page numbers, column widths, line numbers, and header/footer distances, the Section command is a diverse set of formatting commands located in one dialog box. With this command, you can define and format different sections in your document.

To Format a Section in a Document

1. If not already selected, select **Full Menus** from the Edit menu.
2. Move the cursor to the location where you wish to begin a new section.
3. Open the **Format** menu and select **Section**.
4. The Section dialog box will appear, as shown in Figure 37. The formatting selections available in the Section dialog box are described under Options below.

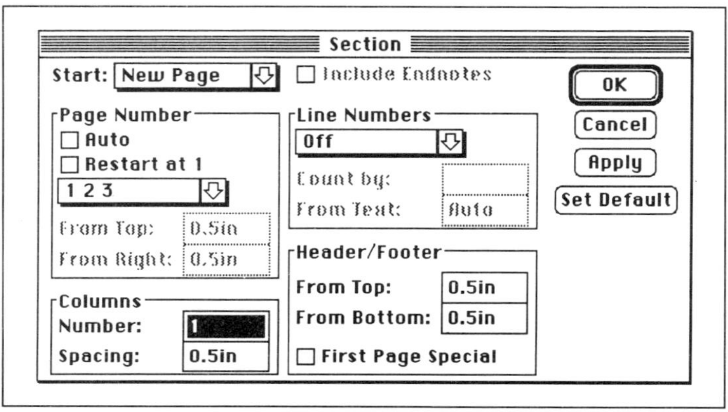

Figure 37: Section dialog box

5. To apply your selections without closing the dialog box, click on **Apply**. To make the current setting the default, select **Set Default**.

6. When you have formatted the section to your satisfaction, click on **OK**, or press **Return**. The selected formatting options will be applied to the document and the dialog box will close. To exit the Section dialog box without applying or saving the changes, click on **Cancel**.

OPTIONS

Start: Defines how and where a section begins. Click on the arrow and drag the mouse down the menu to select from among the following options.

New Page: Begins the section on a new page.

New Column: Begins the section in a new column. The previous and new sections must have the same number of columns; otherwise, the new section will automatically be started on a new page.

No Break: Prevents page breaks from occurring between sections. Footnotes will be embedded within the document at the break point. This option allows you to place different sections with different numbers of columns on the same page.

Even Page: Starts the new section on the next even-numbered page. If the previous section of the document ends on an even-numbered page, Word will insert a blank page between the sections.

Odd Page: Starts the new section on the next odd-numbered page. If the previous section ends on an odd-numbered page, Word will insert a blank page between sections.

Page Number: Defines the placement and format for page numbers in the section.

Auto: Automatically adds page numbers to the section.

Restart at 1: Restarts the page numbering for the section at "1".

1 2 3: Selects standard Arabic numerals for page numbers.

I II III: Selects uppercase Roman numerals for page numbers.

i ii iii: Selects lowercase Roman numerals for page numbers.

A B C: Uses uppercase letters instead of page numbers.

a b c: Uses lowercase letters instead of page numbers.

From Top: Sets the amount of space (in inches) between the top edge of the page and the page number.

From Right: Sets the amount of space (in inches) between the right edge of the page and the page number.

Columns: Sets the number and width of columns in the section. Enter the desired number of columns in the **Number** box. Specify the spacing *between* columns by typing the distance (in inches) in the **Spacing** box.

Include Endnotes: Selecting this option places endnotes at the end of the current section.

Line Numbers: Specifies the type of line numbering (if any) you want included in the section. The line numbers will not appear in Galley View, but will appear in Page View or when you print the document. You can use the following selections to format line numbers:

Off: Turns off line numbering. This is Word's default setting.

By Page: Restarts line numbering at each page break.

By Section: Restarts line numbering at the beginning of the current section.

Continuous: Continues the line numbering from the previous section.

Count by: Sets the increment by which lines will be numbered. For example, you can specify that every fifth line in the section be numbered.

From Text: Specifies the distance from the left margin to the right-most line number, with .25 inch being the default value for single columns, and .13 inch for multiple columns.

Header/Footer: Sets the location of headers and footers in the section. Specify the distance (in inches) between the header or footer and the top or bottom edge of the page in the **From Top** and **From Bottom** boxes, respectively. Click on the **First Page Special** box to suppress headers and footers or to enter different headers and footers on the first page of the section.

See Also *Document, Open Header/Open Footer, Page Setup, Page View, Print Preview*

SEND MAIL

• **MENU** File (Full Menus only)

• **DESCRIPTION** The Send Mail command transmits electronic mail messages between users on an AppleTalk network on which Microsoft Mail has been installed. For additional information on using Microsoft Word on a network, see Appendix A, *Using Microsoft Word on a Network.*

To Send Mail

1. If not already selected, select **Full Menus** from the Edit menu.
2. Open the document or message file you wish to send.
3. Open the **File** menu and select **Send Mail**.
4. A Mail Directory will appear in front of the active document. Select the recipients for the document by clicking on their names.
5. Click on **Send**, or press **Return**. Your document will be delivered to the destinations you have designated.

See Also *Open Mail*

SHADOW

- **MENU** Format

- **DESCRIPTION** The Shadow command adds shadows to characters in your document.

To Create the Shadowed Characters

1. Highlight the characters to which you want to apply the shadowed effect. If you do not specify any text, all subsequently typed characters will be shadowed.
2. Open the **Format** menu and select **Shadow**, or press **⌘-Shift-W**.
3. The selected or new text will appear shadowed.
4. To turn off the shadow effect, select **Shadow** a second time, or select **Plain Text** (**⌘-Shift-Z**).

- **NOTE** All Apple (ImageWriters, ImageWriter II, and LaserWriter Series) and Apple-compatible printers will print shadowed text just as it is displayed on the screen.

See Also *Character*

SHOW CLIPBOARD

- **MENU** Window

- **DESCRIPTION** The Show Clipboard command displays the contents of the Clipboard.

To View the Clipboard

1. Open the **Window** menu and select **Show Clipboard**.
2. The **Clipboard** window will appear in front of the active document window on the Macintosh screen. Note that you cannot edit the contents of the Clipboard.
3. To close the Clipboard, click in the box in the upper left corner of the Clipboard window.

See Also *Copy, Cut*

SHOW RULER/HIDE RULER

• MENU Format

• DESCRIPTION The Ruler allows you to quickly perform a number of formatting actions, including the setting of tab stops, the selection of paragraph formats, and the application of defined styles. Two versions of the ruler are available, depending on the selected menu mode.

To Display the Ruler

1. Open the **Format** menu and select **Show Ruler**, or press **⌘-R**.
2. The Ruler bar will appear along the top of the document window. The options available on the Ruler depend on whether you have selected Short or Full menus. Compare Figures 38 and 39. You can use the various icons, described in the Options section below, to format your document.

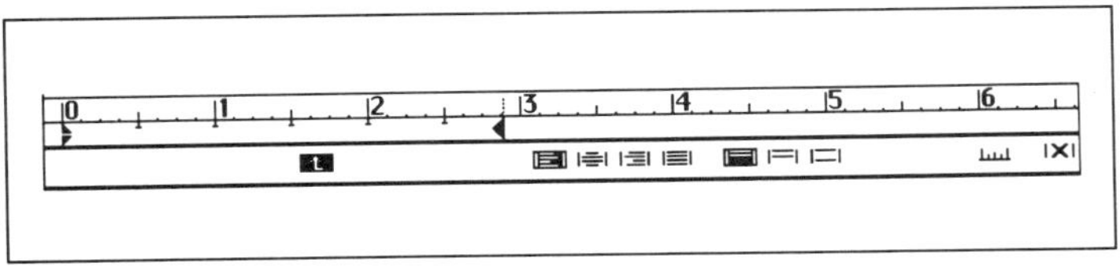

Figure 38: Ruler bar: Short Menus

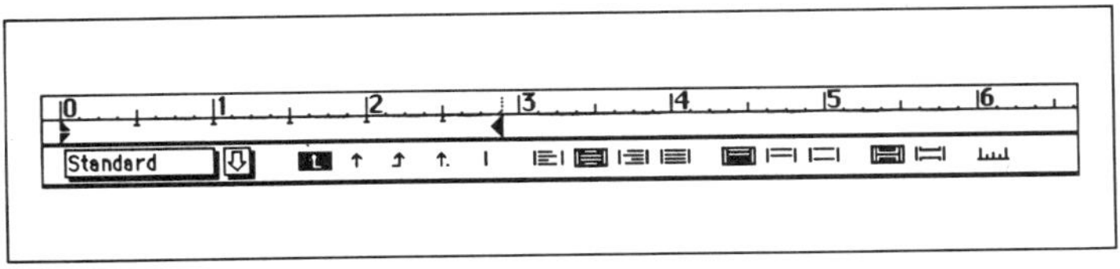

Figure 39: Ruler bar: Full Menus

3. To close the Ruler bar, open the **Format** menu and select **Hide Ruler**.

Options

Style Selection Box: Available only when the Full Menus option is selected, the Style Selection Box is a drop-down menu of paragraph styles. Click on the down arrow and drag the highlight to specify the style of your choice. You will be given the option of modifying the selected style to match the style of the current document, or applying the style as it is.

Indent Markers: These markers denote the position of left (◤), right (◀), and first paragraph line (◣) indentation. To set indentation, click on the desired icon and drag it along the ruler to the desired location.

Tab stop: Sets the positions of tab stops in the selected paragraph. With Full Menus selected, you can select from flush left (↑), centered (↑), flush right (↑), and decimal (↑.) tabs. In the Short Menus version of the rulers, you can select only the flush left tab stop. (For an explanation of the different types of tab stops, see the description of the Tabs option in the *Paragraph* command.) To set tab stops, click on the tab type icon and then click on its desired locations on the ruler.

Vertical line: If the Full Menus mode is selected, the Vertical Line icon (|) will appear on the ruler. Click on the icon and then click on the desired locations on the ruler to embed vertical lines in your paragraphs or between columns.

Alignment icons: Click on these icons to select flush left ( ), centered ( ), flush right ( ), or full ( ) justification.

Line Spacing icons: Sets the line spacing in paragraphs. Select between single ( ), one and a half ( ), or double ( ) spacing.

Open and Close Space icons: Available in the Full Menus mode, the Open Space icon ( ) places 12 points of space before a selected series of paragraphs. Click on the Close Space icon ( ) to delete open space before a series of paragraphs.

Scale icon: The scale icon ( ) sets the scale used by the Ruler. The default scale sets the ruler distance relative to the left margin or column border and shows text column boundaries, tabs, and indents. Clicking on the icon moves to Page scale, with ruler distances set relative to the left page edge and margin locations indicated by left and right brackets ([ ]).

If you have highlighted a table or if the cursor is located within a table, then you can also select Table scale which shows the location of table columns and column boundaries. You can adjust the widths of columns in your table by dragging the indent and column markers to their desired locations on the ruler.

Normal Paragraph icon: Available only when the Short Menus have been selected, clicking on this icon ( ) will revert highlighted or selected paragraphs to Normal (default) style as defined in the Styles box.

• **NOTE** To show the Ruler bar each time you open a document, use the Commands command to put Open Documents With Ruler in the Format menu. Then select **Open Documents With Ruler** once you are back in your document. Word will open all documents with the ruler showing until you turn off Open Document With Ruler command.

See Also *Columns, Commands, Define Styles, Paragraph, Preferences, Save/Save As*

SORT

• **MENU** Utilities (Full Menus only)

• **DESCRIPTION** The Sort command arranges paragraphs in ascending or descending alphabetic order. If you have highlighted a specific body of text, only those paragraphs will be sorted. Otherwise, all paragraphs in the document will be sorted.

To Sort Paragraphs Alphabetically

1. If not already selected, select **Full Menus** from the Edit menu.
2. Highlight the paragraphs to be sorted. If you do not highlight any paragraphs, Sort will reorder every paragraph in the document.
3. Open the **Utilities** menu and select **Sort** to arrange the selection in ascending (A-Z) order. To sort in descending (Z-A) order, hold down the **Shift** key while selecting **Sort**.
4. Word will reorder the selection in ascending (or descending) order.

SPELLING

- **MENU** Utilities

- **DESCRIPTION** The Spelling command verifies the spelling of words in your documents. You can also create and edit your own "user" dictionaries, and access any foreign language dictionaries which have been installed in Microsoft Word.

To Check Spelling

1. Highlight the words, paragraphs, or sections of the document to be checked for proper spelling. If no text is selected, Word assumes that you want to check the spelling of the entire document.
2. Open the **Utilities** menu and select **Spelling**, or press **⌘-L**.
3. The Spelling dialog box will appear, as shown in Figure 40.
4. The dictionaries currently in use will be listed in the **Open Dictionaries** list box. You can add other dictionaries to

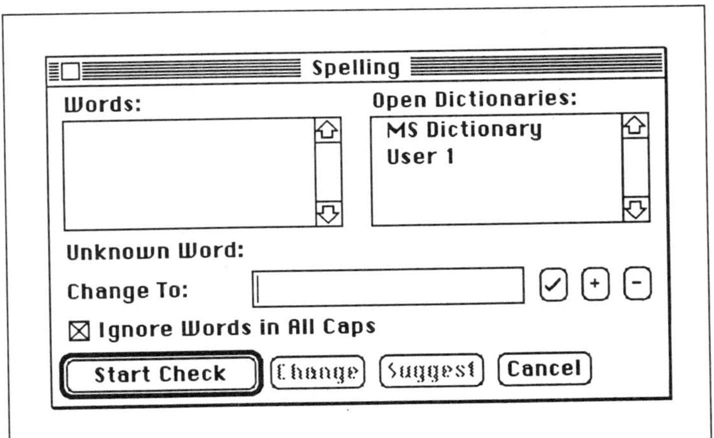

Figure 40: The Spelling dialog box

this box by selecting **Open** from the File menu. To close (remove) a dictionary, click on the dictionary's name and select **Close** from the File menu. To avoid checking the spelling of words which consist of all capital letters, click on the **Ignore Words in All Caps** box. This option is useful for spell checking documents which contain acronyms.

5. Click on **Start Check** to begin searching the document for spelling errors.

6. When the program encounters a word which is not contained in any of the open dictionaries, the word's location in the document will be highlighted and the word will be displayed on the **Unknown Word** line.

7. To get a list of possible spellings, click on the **Suggest** button. The program will display a list of alternatives in the **Words** box. Use the scroll bar, if necessary, to move through the list. To accept a proposed spelling, click on the word in the list box, and then click on **Change** or press **Return**.

8. You can also manually change a word's spelling by typing the correct spelling in the **Change To** box. To make sure that the word in the **Change To** box is spelled correctly, click on the check mark (✓) button. To add the word to the last open User dictionary, click on the plus sign (+) button. To remove the word from the User dictionary, click on the minus sign (–) button.

9. To continue the spell check without changing the word, click on **No Change**.

10. When Word reaches the end of the document in a full document spelling check, it will ask you if you wish to continue checking from the beginning of the document. If the beginning of the document has already been checked, Word will tell you that it has completed the spelling check. Click on **OK** to continue editing your document. To cancel the spelling check prior to its completion, click on **Cancel**.

See Also *Change, Find, Find Again*

STYLES

• MENU Format (Full Menus only)

• DESCRIPTION The Styles command applies preset paragraph and character formats to selected paragraphs. Use the Styles command to enhance the overall appearance of paragraphs in your document.

To Apply a Style to a Paragraph

1. If not already selected, select **Full Menus** from the Edit menu.
2. Highlight the paragraphs to which you want to apply a specific style.
3. Open the **Format** menu and select **Styles**.
4. The Styles dialog box will appear.
5. Select the style to be used by clicking on its name in the list box. A description of the style will appear in the box below the list box.
6. To apply the style immediately without closing the Styles dialog box, click on **Apply**.
7. When you are satisfied with the style, click on **OK**. The specified paragraph and character formats will be applied to the selected text.
8. To close the Styles dialog box, click on the small box in the upper left corner of the dialog box, or click on **Cancel**. Any

styles added to your document with the **Apply** button will *not* be cancelled.

• NOTE Holding down the Shift Key while selecting the Styles command will display all of Word's automatic styles in the Styles command list box.

See Also *Character, Define Styles, Paragraph, Show Ruler/Hide Ruler*

TABLE

• MENU Edit (Full Menus only)

• DESCRIPTION The Table command modifies the structure of an existing table in your document.

To Change a Table's Structure

1. If not already selected, select **Full Menus** from the Edit menu.
2. Highlight the table or cells you want to modify. You can shift, merge, or split table cells and add or delete rows and columns.
3. Open the **Edit** menu and select **Table**.
4. The Table dialog box will appear, as shown in Figure 41.
5. Modify the format of the table by clicking on the relevant buttons. The functions of each of the buttons are explained

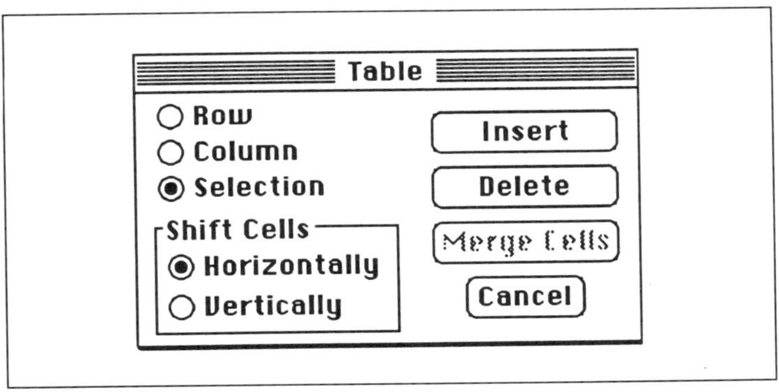

Figure 41: Table dialog box

in the Options section below. The Table dialog box will automatically disappear from the screen when an action is taken.

6. To cancel the Table command, click on the **Cancel** button.

OPTIONS

Insert: This option inserts rows, columns, or cells into the table. Specify whether you wish to insert a **Row**, **Column**, or a **Selection** of cells by clicking on the appropriate button. Your selection in the Shift Cells box will determine how the surrounding cells of the table will realign themselves.

Delete: This option deletes rows, columns, or cells. Specify whether you wish to delete a **Row**, **Column**, or **Selection** of cells by clicking on the appropriate radio button. Your selection in the Shift Cells box will determine how the surrounding cells of the table will realign themselves.

Merge Cells: Removes the boundaries between a row of selected cells to create one large horizontal cell. This option can only merge across rows.

Split Cell: This option splits previously merged cells.

Shift Cells: Specifies the direction cells will shift after cells are inserted or deleted. This feature is available only if the Selection button is chosen. Selecting **Horizontally** will shift cells to the right, if you are inserting cells, or to the left, if you are deleting cells. Selecting **Vertically** shifts cells down, if cells are being inserted, or up, if cells are being deleted.

See Also *Cells, Insert Table*

TABLE OF CONTENTS

- **MENU** Utilities (Full Menus only)

- **DESCRIPTION** The Table of Contents command compiles a table of contents for your document using either the embedded contents codes (*.c.*) or the heading entries from the Outlining command.

To Compile a Table Of Contents

1. If not already selected, select **Full Menus** from the Edit menu.
2. Use the Insert TOC Entry command to place the contents code (*.c.*) before the text that you want added to the table of contents.

   To make a table of contents from an outline, create an outline for your document by using the Outlining command.
3. Open the **Utilities** menu and select **Table of Contents**.
4. The Table of Contents dialog box will appear.
5. Indicate the source of table of contents entries by clicking on **Outline** for a document outline or **.c. Paragraphs** for TOC entries. You can control the depth of the table of contents (that is, the number of subheadings listed) by clicking on the **All** button or specifying a range in the **From** and **To** boxes. You can designate up to nine levels of subheadings.
6. To include page numbers in the table of contents, click on **Show Page Numbers**.

7. Click on **Start** to begin compiling the table of contents, or **Cancel** to leave the Table of Contents dialog box. Once the compilation of the table of contents has begun, you may press **⌘-.** (period) to cancel the process.

8. The completed table of contents will appear at the beginning of your document.

See Also *Insert TOC Entry, Outlining*

TABLE TO TEXT

• **MENU** Document (Full Menus only)

• **DESCRIPTION** The Table to Text command converts table rows into text rows.

To Convert a Table into Text

1. If not already selected, select **Full Menus** from the Edit menu.
2. Highlight the table rows to be converted to text.
3. Open the **Document** menu and select **Table To Text**.
4. The Table To Text dialog box will appear.
5. Specify the conversion type. **Paragraph** makes each table cell a separate paragraph. **Tab delimited** separates the contents of each cell with a tab and makes each row a separate paragraph. **Comma delimited** separates each cell with a comma and makes each row a separate paragraph.
6. After selecting the conversion type, click on **OK**. The selected table rows will be converted to text.

See Also *Insert Table, Table*

UNDERLINE

• **MENU** Format

• **DESCRIPTION** The Underline command toggles the underlining of characters.

To Underline Characters

1. Highlight the text you want to underline. If you do not specify text, the underlining will be applied to subsequently typed text.
2. Open the **Format** menu and select **Underline**, or press **⌘-Shift-U**.
3. The highlighted or subsequently typed text will be underlined. To turn off the underlining, select **Underline** again.

See Also *Character*

UNDO/REDO

• **MENU** Edit

• **DESCRIPTION** Undo reverses the last command issued. Many Word commands are reversible, and if the preceding command is one, its name will be shown next to the Undo command in the Edit Menu. After you select Undo, its name on the menu will change to Redo until you issue another command.

To Undo a Command

1. Open the **Edit** menu and select **Undo**, or press **⌘-Z**.
2. The immediately preceding command will be reversed.
3. To revert back to the result of the original command (*i.e.,* to "undo" the Undo command), select **Redo** from the Edit menu, or press **⌘-Z**.

• **NOTE** The following Microsoft Word commands *cannot* be reversed with the Undo command:

All commands from the File menu

All commands from the Window menu

Calculate

Commands

Document

Find

Go To

Outlining

Preferences

Repaginate Now

Spelling

UPDATE LINK

• **MENU** Edit (Full Menus only)

• **DESCRIPTION** The Update Link command updates information from another application which has been linked to your document with Word's QuickSwitch Utility.

Using the Update Link Command

1. If not already selected, select **Full Menus** from the Edit menu.
2. Highlight the linked information.
3. Open the **Edit** menu and select **Update Link**. The linked information will be updated.
4. If Word cannot find the file that has been linked to your document, a dialog box will appear, stating that the file cannot be found (Figure 42). Use the options in the dialog box to navigate through the folders on your hard or floppy disks and find the linked application and file.

See Also *Edit Link, Paste Link*

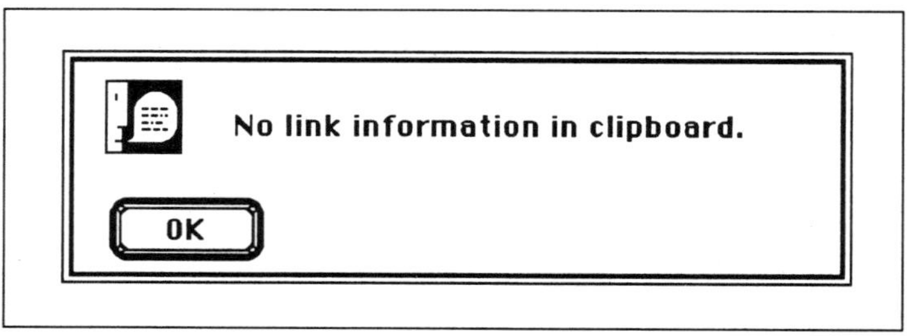

Figure 42: Update Link (Cannot Find) dialog box

WORD COUNT

- **MENU** Utilities (Full Menus only)

- **DESCRIPTION** The Word Count command counts characters, words, lines, or paragraphs in your documents. Word Count will also count items within the main text and footnotes of your document, or in a selected range of text, but will not count text in headers and footers.

To Count Words in Your Document

1. If not already selected, select **Full Menus** from the Edit menu.
2. Highlight the text in which you want to complete a count. If you do not specify a text selection, Word will automatically perform the count throughout the entire document.
3. Open the **Utilities** menu and select **Word Count**.
4. The Word Count dialog box will appear, as shown in Figure 43.

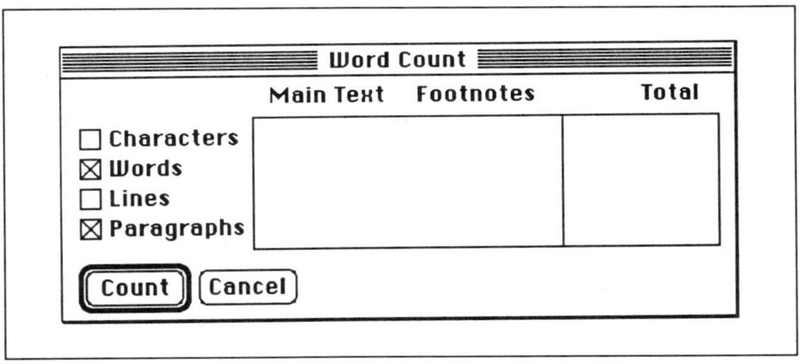

Figure 43: Word Count dialog box

5. Specify whether you wish to tabulate **Characters, Words, Lines, Paragraphs,** or any combination of items.
6. Click on the **Start** button. Word will begin to tabulate on-screen the items you specified. The progress of the tabulation will be indicated by the percentage in the lower right corner of the dialog box.
7. Click on **Stop** to interrupt the tabulation. You can restart the count by clicking on **Count**.
8. Click on **Cancel** to stop the count and close the Word Count dialog box.

APPENDIX A
Using Microsoft Word on a Network

Microsoft Word 4.0 for the Macintosh has been designed for use on AppleTalk and compatible networks. Microsoft sells a separate electronic mail product, Microsoft Mail, for sending messages between Microsoft Word users on an AppleTalk network. For additional information on using Microsoft Mail, see the command references for *Open Mail* and *Send Mail*, and consult your User's Manual.

Network Considerations for Using Microsoft Word

Several factors can affect the performance of Microsoft Word on a network. First, the relative level of network traffic affects the speed with which a document reaches the printer. Second, the size of your file and the number of character enhancements determine how quickly your document will print. Third, running Word from a central file server affects the speed of command execution. Finally, the use of print spoolers on your system allows you to continue working on your Macintosh while you are waiting for documents to print on the central printer.

Network Traffic: When transferring large files across a network, consider the relative level of network traffic. Peak periods of traffic on the network will increase the amount of time required to transfer your file from one location to another.

The status screens provided with Macintosh network products include indicators of network traffic. The file server screen typically displays the status of network traffic with a bar graph or some other indicator. Before sending lengthy documents to another Macintosh or to a shared printer, check the activity level of the network to gauge the amount of time needed to transfer or print your document.

Size of Files: The size of the document you are sending to a networked printer will have a great effect on the total amount of time the print process takes. Keep in mind that once your job reaches the queue in the printer's memory, the printer will re-compose each page of your document in its memory so that it can print the document. This process can take quite a while for documents larger than 10 pages. As a general rule, you should send large files over the network only when the relative activity level of the network is less than 35 percent of capacity. If network activity exceeds 35 percent, consider sending your document in smaller segments.

Character and Font Enhancements in Documents: When documents are sent to a networked printer, the printer must define the document's character and font enhancements and then image them onto a page. If you want to print a file which requires much special formatting (such as three or more fonts on one page or imported graphics files embedded in the text), you should wait until the activity level of the network is low so that your document will print faster and avoid tying up the network.

Location of Microsoft Word on the Network: It takes longer to create, edit, save, and print documents if you are accessing Word from a remote file server than if you run Word on your own machine. With Microsoft Word readily accessible from your hard disk, you can complete frequent disk accesses, use Microsoft Mail to send and receive messages from other Word users on your network, and use print spoolers to save your documents in your system's background memory. If Microsoft Word is shared over a centralized file server, it will take more time to edit your documents since you must wait for the Word commands to travel over the network to the file server and back to your machine.

Using Print Spoolers: Print spoolers are very useful for printing documents over a network. A print spooler intercepts your Microsoft Word document before it reaches the printer and stores it on your hard disk. When the networked printer is available, the spooler will automatically send the document to the printer. While this is happening, your Macintosh is still free for you to use.

Print spoolers can either be installed on the network file server or on your Macintosh system, but you achieve the best results with Microsoft Word if the print spooler is installed on your Macintosh. Apple's Print Monitor is an excellent spooler and is included with every Macintosh. Keep in mind, though, that Print Monitor is only compatible with Apple (LaserWriter, SC, ImageWriter, ImageWriter II, etc.) printers. Several Apple software developers have created print spoolers that perform well on networked Macintosh systems. SuperMac's LaserSpool is easy to install and use. Contact your Apple dealer for more information on this or other print spoolers. Microsoft tests many third party print drivers and print spoolers to ensure their compatibility with Word.

To use a spooler, select the Spooler icon in the Chooser dialog box under the Apple menu, and then begin your print job.

Additional Network Suggestions

1. Install Microsoft Word on the most heavily used machines on your network. If many Macintoshes on your network require Microsoft Word, call Microsoft Corporation at (206) 882-8080 for information on obtaining a site license. If only a few of your machines require a copy of Word, it may be more economical to purchase additional copies of Word from your local computer dealer.

2. If you have not yet installed a network, you should consider using TOPS (from Sitka) due to its speed of file transfer and its print spooling capability. TOPS is the market leader in low-cost local area network operating systems for the Macintosh.

3. The majority of network time is occupied by printing. As new users are added to your network, consider adding additional printers to ease the flow of network traffic resulting from printing tasks.

APPENDIX B

Short Menus Versus Full Menus

Microsoft Word provides you with the option of selecting Short or Full command menus. Short Menus provide you with the commands that are essential for document creation, editing, saving, and printing, while Full Menus give you complete access to all Word commands. You may switch between the menu types by selecting **Short Menus** or **Full Menus** in the Edit menu. By default, Word starts each session with Short Menus.

The following commands are available only with Full Menus.

File Menu

Delete

Open Mail

Send Mail

Edit Menu

Commands

Glossary

Paste Link

Preferences

Table

Update Link

Format Menu

Cells

Character

Define Styles

Paragraph

Plain For Style

Position
Section
Styles

Document Menu

Insert Graphics
Insert Index Entry
Insert Table
Insert TOC Entry
Open Even Footer
Open Even Header
Open First Footer
Open First Header
Open Odd Footer
Open Odd Header
Outlining

Utilities Menu

Calculate
Go Back
Hyphenate
Index
Renumber
Sort
Table of Contents
Word Count

Window Menu

New Window

Full Menus also provide you with the following additional features:

Split windows.
Additional keystroke command shortcuts.
Additional tab types and spacing options.

Mouse shortcuts for moving, cutting, and pasting text.

The following commands have additional options when used in Full Menus mode (see the specific command reference for further details):

Document

Footnote

Open Header/Open Footer

Save As

APPENDIX C

Microsoft Word Command Quick Reference

Microsoft Word 4.0 includes numerous formatting, entry, and cursor movement commands which are not included on the menus. There is not enough space in the confines of this book to look at each of these commands in depth. Many of these commands are self-explanatory and do not require further discussion. Also, there are times when you don't need a full explanation of a command's features but only want a quick reminder of a particular command's menu location or keystroke sequence.

The two lists in this appendix provide you with a handy quick reference to the most frequently used formats, fonts, and movement commands. Each command is listed with its default keystroke sequence and menu location. Please note that "Command" refers to the ⌘ key on the Macintosh keyboard. For more information about any of the commands listed here, please refer to the specific command reference in this book or to your *Microsoft Word User's Guide.*

Each font in the font list is presented along with sample text in the indicated point size. These fonts were printed on a QMS-PS 810 laser printer. The fonts available for your laser printer may vary. Check the manual for your specific model of printer for more details.

Commands

Command	Keystroke Combinations	Menu
9 Point		Font
10 Point		Font
12 Point		Font
14 Point		Font
18 Point		Font
24 Point		Font
Activate Key-board Menus	Command - Tab *or* Keypad . (period)	
Add to Menu	Command - Option - = *or* Command - Shift - Option - =	
Again	Command - A	Edit
All Caps	Command - Shift - K *or* Shift - F10	
Assign to Key	Command - Option - Keypad + *or* Command - Shift - Option - Left Arrow	
Backspace	Delete	
Bold	Command - Shift - B *or* F10	Format
Calculate	Command - =	Utilities

Command	Keystroke Combinations	Menu
Cancel	Clear *or* Command - (period)	
Cells...		Format
Centered	Command - Shift - C	
Change Font	Command - Shift - E	
Change Style	Command - Shift - S	
Change...	Command - H	Utilities
Character...	Command - D *or* F14	Format
Clear		Edit
Close	Command - W	File
Commands...		Edit
Context Sensitive Help	Command - / *or* help	
Copy	Command - C *or* F3	Edit
Copy as Picture	Command - Option - D	
Copy Formats	Command - Option - V *or* Shift - F4	

Command	Keystroke Combinations	Menu
Copy Text	Command - Option - C *or* Shift - F3	
Cut	Command - X *or* F2	Edit
Define Styles...	Command - T	Format
Delete Forward	Command - Option - F *or* del	
Delete Next Word	Command - Option - G	
Delete Previous Word	Command - Option - delete	
Delete...		File
Document...	Command - F14	Format
Dotted Underline	Command - Shift - \ *or* Option - F12	
Double Space	Command - Shift - Y	
Double Underline	Command - Shift - [*or* Shift - F12	

Command	Keystroke Combinations	Menu
Edit Link (Quickswitch)	Command - (comma) *or* Option - F2	
Extend to Character	Command - Option - H *or* Keypad - (minus sign)	
Find Again	Command - Option - A *or* Keypad =	Utilities
Find Formats	Command - Option - R	
Find...	Command - F	Utilities
First Line Indent	Command - Shift - F	
Flush Left	Command - Shift - L	
Flush Right	Command - Shift - R	
Footnote...	Command - E	Document
Glossary...	Command - K	Edit
Go Back	Command - Option - Z *or* Keypad 0	Utilities
Go To...	Command - G	Utilities
Hanging Indent	Command - Shift - T	
Help...		Window

Command	Keystroke Combinations	Menu
Hidden Text	Command - Shift - V *or* Command - Shift - X *or* Option - F9	
Hyphenate...	Shift - F15	Utilities
Index...		Utilities
Insert Formula	Command - Option - \	
Insert Glossary Text	Command - Delete	
Insert Graphics		Document
Insert Index Entry		Document
Insert Line Break	Shift - Return	
Insert New Paragraph	Return *or* Enter	
Insert New Section	Command - Enter	
Insert Nonbreaking Hyphen	Command -	
Insert Nonbreaking Space	Option - Spacebar *or* Command - Spacebar	
Insert Optional Hyphen	Command - (hyphen)	

Command	Keystroke Combinations	Menu
Insert Page Break	Shift - Enter	Document
Insert Tab	Tab *or* Option - Tab	
Insert TOC Entry		Document
Insert ¶ Above Row	Command - Option - Spacebar	
Italic	Command - Shift - I *or* F11	Format
Justified	Command - Shift - J	
L Thick Paragraph Border	Command - Option - 2	
Larger Font Size	Command - Shift - (period) *or* Command - Shift - >	
More Keyboard Prefix	Command - Option - '	
Move Down One Text Area	Command - Option - Keypad 2	
Move Left One Text Area	Command - Option - Keypad 4	
Move Right OneText Area	Command - Option - Keypad 6	
Move Text	Command - Option - X *or* Shift - F2	

Command	Keystroke Combinations	Menu
Move to Bottom of Window	end	
Move to End of Document	Command - Keypad - 3	
Move to End of Document	Command - end	
Move to End of Line	Keypad 1	
Move to First Text Area	Command - Option - Keypad 7	
Move to Last Text Area	Command - Option - Keypad 1	
Move to Next Character	Right Arrow *or* Command - Option - L *or* Keypad 6	
Move to Next Line	Down Arrow *or* Command-Option-(comma) *or* Keypad 2	
Move to Next Page	Command - page down	

Command	Keystroke Combinations	Menu
Move to Next Paragraph	Command - Down *or* Command - Option - B *or* Command - Keypad 2	
Move to Next Sentence	Command - Keypad 1	
Move to Next Text Area	Command - Option - Keypad 3	
Move to Next Window	Command - Option - W	
Move to Next Word	Command - Right Arrow *or* Command - Option - ; *or* Command - Keypad 6	
Move to Previous Cell	Shift - Tab	
Move to Previous Character	Left Arrow *or* Command - Option - K *or* Keypad 4	

Command	Keystroke Combinations	Menu
Move to Previous Line	Up Arrow *or* Command - Option - O *or* Keypad 8	
Move to Previous Page	Command - page up	
Move to Previous Paragraph	Command - Up Arrow *or* Command - Option - Y *or* Command - Keypad - 8	
Move to Previous Sentence	Command - Keypad 7	
Move to Previous Text Area	Command - Option - Keypad 9	
Move to Previous Word	Command - Left Arrow *or* Command - Option - J *or* Command - Keypad 4	

Command	Keystroke Combinations	Menu
Move to Start of Document	Command - Keypad 9 *or* Command - home	
Move to Start of Line	Keypad 7	
Move to Top of Window	Command - Keypad 5 *or* home	
Move Up One Text Area	Command - Option - Keypad 8	
Nest Paragraph	Command - Shift - N	
New	Command - N *or* F5	File
New Window	Shift - F5	Window
New ¶ After Insertion Point	Command - Option - Return	
New ¶ with Same Style	Command - Return	
No Paragraph Border	Command - Option - 1	
Normal Paragraph	Command - Shift - P	
Numeric Lock	Keypad Clear	
Open Any File...	Shift - F6	
Open Footer...		Document
Open Footnote Window	Command - Shift - Option - S	
Open Header...		Document
Open Mail...		File
Open Spacing	Command - Shift - O	

Command	Keystroke Combinations	Menu
Open...	Command - O *or* F6	File
Outline	Command - Shift - D *or* Shift -F11	Format
Outline Command Prefix	Command - Option - T	
Outlining	Command - U *or* Shift - F13	Document
Page Setup...	Shift - F8	File
Page View	Command - B *or* F13	Document
Paragraph...	Command - M *or* Shift - F14	Format
Paste	Command - V *or* F4	Edit
Paste Link	Option - F4	Edit
Paste Special Character	Command - Option - Q	

Command	Keystroke Combinations	Menu
Plain For Style	Command - Shift - Spacebar *or* F9	Format
Plain Text	Command - Shift - Z *or* Shift - F9	Format
Position...		Format
Preferences...		Edit
Print Merge...		File
Print Preview...	Command - I *or* Option - F13	File
Print...	Command - P *or* F8	File
Quit	Command - Q	File
Remove From Menu	Command - Option - (hyphen)	
Renumber...	Command - F15	Utilities
Repaginate Now	Command - J	Document
Save	Command - S *or* F7	File
Save As...	Shift - F7	File

Command	Keystroke Combinations	Menu
Scroll Line Down	Command - Option - / *or* Keypad +	
Scroll Line Up	Command - Option - [*or* Keypad *	
Scroll Screen Down	Command - Option - (period) *or* Keypad 3 *or* page down	
Scroll Screen Up	Command - Option - P *or* Keypad 9 *or* page up	
Section...	Option - F14	Format
Select Whole Document	Command - Option - M	
Send Mail...		File
Shadow	Command - Shift - W *or* Option - F11	Format

Command	Keystroke Combinations	Menu
Short Menus		Edit
Show Clipboard		Window
Show/Hide Ruler	Command - R	Format
Show/Hide ¶	Command - Y	Edit
Small Caps	Command - Shift - H *or* Option - F10	
Smaller Font Size	Command - Shift - < *or* Command - Shift - (comma)	
Sort		Utilities
Spelling...	Command - L *or* F15	Utilities
Split Window	Command - Option - S	
Strikethru	Command - Shift - /	
Styles...		Format
Subscript 2 pt	Command - Shift - (hyphen)	
Superscript 3 pt	Command - Shift - =	
Symbol Font	Command - Shift - Q	
Table of Contents...		Utilities
Table to Text...		Document
Table...		Edit
Underline	Command - Shift - U *or* F12	Format

Command	Keystroke Combinations	Menu
Undo	Command - Z *or* F1	Edit
Unnest Paragraph	Command - Shift - M	
Untitled1		Window
Untitled2		Window
Update Link	Option - F3	Edit
Word Count...	Option - F15	Utilities
Word Underline	Command - Shift -] *or* Command - F12	
Zoom Window	Command - Option -]	

Fonts

Font Name	Size	Sample Text
AGaramond	12 pt.	ABCDE abcde 12345
AGaramond Bold	12 pt.	**ABCDE abcde 12345**
AGaramond Bold Italic	12 pt.	***ABCDE abcde 12345***
AGaramond Italic	12 pt.	*ABCDE abcde 12345*
AGaramond Semibold	12 pt.	ABCDE abcde 12345
AGaramond Semibold Italic	12 pt.	*ABCDE abcde 12345*
Avant Garde	12 pt.	ABCDE abcde 12345
B Garamond Bold	14 pt.	**ABCDE abcde 12345**
BI Garamond Bold Italic	14 pt.	***ABCDE abcde 12345***
Bookman	12 pt.	ABCDE abcde 12345
Chicago	12 pt.	**ABCDE abcde 12345**
Courier	12 pt.	ABCDE abcde 12345
Garamond	12 pt.	ABCDE abcde 12345
Geneva	12 pt.	ABCDE abcde 12345
Helvetica	12 pt.	ABCDE abcde 12345
Monaco	12 pt.	ABCDE abcde 12345
N Helvetica Narrow	12 pt.	ABCDE abcde 12345
New Century Schoolbook	12 pt.	ABCDE abcde 12345
New York	12 pt.	ABCDE abcde 12345
Palatino	12 pt.	ABCDE abcde 12345
Symbol	12 pt.	ΑΒΧΔΕ αβχδε 12345
Times	12 pt.	ABCDE abcde 12345
Zapf Chancery	12 pt.	*ABCDE abcde 12345*
Zapf Dingbats	12 pt.	✡✣✤✥✦ ❁❂❃❄❅ ➾➽✓✔✗

Index

+ (addition or plus sign)
  as mathematical operator, 8
  used to add words to dictionary, 128
  used with Outlining command, 76, 77
[ ] (brackets), 125
: (colon), 61
, (comma), 41, 103
/ (division operator), 8
... (ellipses), 87
= (equal to), 104
! (exclamation point), 91
> (greater than), 104
>= (greater than or equal to), 104
«» (guillemets), 103
< (less than), 104
<= (less than or equal to), 104
- (minus or subtraction sign), 76, 77, 128
  mathematical operator, 8
* (multiplication operator), 8
<> (not equal to), 104
() (parentheses), 8
  in arrays, 41
  in calculations, 8
  in Displace options, 42
% (percentage operator), 8
" (quotation marks), 98
; (semicolon), 61

About command (Apple menu), 1
acronyms, avoiding the spell checking of, 128
addition or plus sign (+)
  as mathematical operator, 8
  used with Outlining command, 76, 77
  used to add words to dictionary, 128
Again command (Edit menu), 2
Align Rows option, 10
alignment, icons for, 124
alphabetizing, 126
Apple printers. *See* ImageWriter printers; LaserWriter printers; printers
AppleTalk networks, 15–16, 73, 141–143
applications, external
  accesssing from Word, 34
  linking information from, 90–91
  updating information from, 138
Arabic numerals
  for paragraphs, 108–110
  for section page numbers, 118
arrays, formatting of, 41–42
ascending sort order, 126
ASCII (plain text) files, 71, 114

Background Repagination option, 98, 111
backing up files, automatic, 113
Backspace key, 17
bars, vertical, 87, 124
Beneath Text footnote option, 31
binding, margins for, 29–30
Bold command (Format menu), 3
boldface, 3
  resetting, 92, 93
  when printing in draft mode, 102
borders. *See also* graphic frames
  for cells, 4–5
  hairline, 6
  for paragraphs, 5–6
Borders command, 4–6
Borders dialog box, 4, 6
  accessing from Paragraph dialog box, 88
Bottom of Page footnote option, 31
boundaries
  setting with Position command, 95
  showing, 106
Box formula command, 45
boxes
  cell, 5–6
  formula, 45
  hollow, 77
  paragraph, 4–5
Bracket formula command, 42
bracketing mathematical expressions, 42
brackets ([ ]), used on ruler, 125
By Example numbering option, 110

Calculate command (Utilities menu), 7–8, 137
calculations, 7–8, 137
calendar icon, 72
capitalization. *See* letters, uppercase
cells. *See also* columns
  borders for, 4, 5–6
  defining height of, 10
  formatting, 9–10
  modifying, 131–132
Cells command (Edit menu), 9–10
Change command (Utilities menu), 11
Character command (Format menu), 12–14, 91
character string searches, 35, 36

character style
  boldface, 3, 92, 93, 102
  outlined, 75
  resetting, 92
  shadowed, 121
  underlining, 13, 136
characters
  counting, 139–140
  displacing, 42
  formatting, 12–14
  hiding/showing, 54–55
  matching capitalization of, in searches, 11, 35
  overstriking, 42, 44
  separator, 109
  style sheets for, 26–27
Chooser command (Apple menu), 15–16, 82
Clear command (Edit menu), 17
Clipboard, 59, 122
  calculations in, 7
  used for copying, 24
  used for cutting, 25
clock icon, 72
Close command (File menu), 18
Close Space ruler icon, 124
closing
  documents, 18
  windows, 69
codes. *See* hidden characters; hidden text
colon (:), in index entries, 61
Color character option, 14
colors of text, 14
Column Width option, 65
columns
  formatting, 19–20, 118
  formatting arrays in, 42
  new, in section, 117
  previous settings of, 10
  snaking, 19–20
  in tables, 65, 132
  widths of, 10, 65
Columns command, 19–20, 118
Comma Delimited table option, 65
command configuration files
  identifying, 23
  restoring, 23
  updating current, 22
commands
  creating list of, 23
  customizing, 21–23
  repeating, 2
  undoing, 137
Commands command (Edit menu), 21–23, 137
commas (,)
  delineating numbers with, 41
  in data documents, 103
Convert From table option, 65
converting
  files, 113–115
  table rows to text, 135
  text to table rows, 65
Copies print option, 100
Copy command (Edit menu), 24, 90
copying
  from other applications, 90
  graphic images, 24
  text, 24
counting, 139–140
Cover Page print option, 102
cover pages, 102
cropping graphic images, 59–60
cursor, moving to previous points, 50
Custom Paper Size setup option, 99
customizing commands, 21–23
Cut command (Edit menu), 25
cutting. *See also* deleting, pasting
  graphic images, 25
  text, 25

dashed lines, 87
data documents, for print merging, 103–105
date
  in documents, 48
  in header or footer, 72
Date header/footer option, 72
decimal tabs, 87, 124
Default Measure setup option, 97
default settings
  for boxes, 45
  for columns in arrays, 42
  in command configuration files, 23
  defining, 97–99
  for menus on start-up, 46
  for page viewing, 84
  for paragraph numbering, 109
  setting of with style sheets, 27
  of space between columns, 65
  of spacing value, 5
  and standard glossary, 48
  of tab stops, setting, 31
Default Tab Stops document option, 31
Define Styles command (Format menu), 26–27, 71

Delete command (File menu), 28
Delete key, 17
Delete table option, 132
deleting
  documents, 28
  rows, columns, and cells from tables, 132
  text, 17
descending sort order, 126
dictionaries
  adding words to, 128
  creating new, 68
  in use, 127
  opening new, 127–128
  using Open command with, 71
disk drive selection, 28, 113
Displace formula option, 42
Distance From Text position option, 95
division symbol (/), 8
Do command option, 22
Document command (Format menu), 29–33, 137
Document page setup option, 81–82
documents. *See also* files; text
  adding to menus, 23
  closing, 18
  creating backups of, 113
  creating second windows for, 69
  data or text, for print merges, 103–105
  deleting, 28
  field options for, 104–105
  inserting glossary entries into, 48–49
  opening new, 68
  opening with ruler, 125
  opening saved, 70–71
  outlining, 76–79
  replacing contents of, 113
  saving, 18, 112–115
  updating linked, 138
dotted underlining, 13
double spacing, 124
Draft print option, 102
drive selection, 28, 113

Edit Link command (Edit menu), 34, 90
editing
  Clipboard contents, 122
  in Page View, 19
ejecting floppy disks, 28, 70
electronic mail messages, 73–74, 120
ellipses (...), 87
embedded characters. *See* hidden characters
End of Section footnote option, 31, 33
endnotes. *See* footnotes
enhancements, character, 12–14
  adding, 94
enlarging documents, 82
equations, formatting, 41–45
Even Page section option, 117
even-numbered pages, starting section on, 117
Even/Odd header/footer option, 30
Excel (Microsoft), linking information from, 91
exclamation point (!), used in links, 91

Fast Save option, 113
Faster Bitmap Printing option, 82
fields
  in data documents, 103
  options for, 104–105
File Format save option, 114–115
files. *See also* documents
  comma-delimited, 65
  converting to other formats, 113–115
  opening, 70–71
  revising, from other applications, 34
  tab-delimited, 65
Find Again command (Utilities menu), 36
Find command (Utilities menu), 2, 35, 137
floppy disks, changing/ejecting, 70, 113
folders, changing, 70, 113
Font menu, 37–38
Font character option, 13
Font Substitution Page setup option, 82
Font/DA Mover, 45, 82
fonts. *See also* boldface; italics
  changing, 37–38
  modifying with Character command, 12–14
  non-standard, effect on printing, 14
  spacing of, during printing, 82
  substituting, 82
  units of measurement of, 97
Footer (Header/) section option, 119
footers
  creating, 72
  exclusion from word count, 139
  setting location of, 119
  suppressing, 119

Footnote command (Document menu), 39–40
footnotes
adding, 39–40
at end of section, 118
at section break points, 117
changing position of, 32–33
counting words in, 139–140
numbering options, 31
Footnotes document option, 31
form letters, 103–105
formulas. *See* mathematical formulas
Fraction formula option, 43
Fractional Widths page setup option, 82
fractions, 43
Full Menus, contents of, 145–147
Full Menus command, 46

Galley View, 19, 84
and Position command, 96
global changes, 11
glossaries
creating entries for, 47–48
creating new, 68
default, 48
inserting entries from, 48–49
Open command with, 71
printing, 102
Glossary command (Edit menu), 47–49, 68, 71
Go Back command (Utilities menu), 50
Go To command (Utilities menu), 51, 137
graphic frames
duplicating, 60
enhancing, 60
re-sizing, 59–60
graphic images
copying, 24
cropping, 59–60
cutting, 25
inserting, 59–60, 89
placeholders for, 98
placing, 94–95
printing extra-high quality, 82
printing PostScript files of, 82
Graphics Smoothing option, 82
gridlines in tables, displaying, 98
guillemets («»), creating, 103
Gutter document option, 30

Hand Feed print option, 101
Header/Footer section option, 119
headers
creating, 72
exclusion from word count, 139
page numbering in, 30
setting even/odd, 30
setting location of, 119
suppressing, 119
heading entries, for outline, 76–78
used with Table of Contents command, 133
height of cells, setting 10
help, online, 1, 52–53
Help command (Window menu), 52–53
Help commands option, 22
hidden characters, 61
hiding, 54–55
for index entries, 61–62, 101
for linking information, 91
printing, 98, 101
showing, 54–55, 66, 98
for table of contents, 66, 133
hidden text
in page length calculations, 111
printing, 101
showing, 98
Hide ¶ command (Edit menu), 54–55
Hide Ruler command (Format menu), 123–125
hierarchical text placement. *See* outlines
Horizontal position option, 95
Hyphenate command (Utilities menu), 56–57
hyphens, 54, 56–57

ImageWriter printers, 15
Page Setup dialog box for, 81
Print dialog box for, 101
printing quality of, 102
selecting paper size for, 99
selecting paper source for, 100
selecting paper types for, 80
shadowed text with, 121
importing
files, 113–115
text into columns, 65
In Line position option, 95
Include Endnotes section option, 118
indent markers, 124
Indent Rows cells option, 10
indention
icons on ruler, 124
of paragraphs, 86
of rows, 10
Indents paragraph option, 86

Index Characters index option, 58
Index command (Utilities menu), 58
indexes, 58
  creating multiple level, 61
  marking entries for, 61–62
  Next File document option for, 31
  printing entry codes, 101
Insert Graphics command (Document menu), 59–60
Insert Index Entry command (Document menu), 61–62
Insert Page Break command (Document menu), 63
Insert Table command (Document menu), 64–65
Insert TOC Entry command (Document menu), 66, 133
Insert table option, 132
inserting
  entries in indexes, 61
  graphic images, 89
  page breaks, 63
  rows, columns, cells into tables, 132
  text, 89
Inside position option, 95
Integral formula option, 43
italics, 67
  resetting, 92, 93
  when printing in draft mode, 102
Italics command (Format menu), 67

justification, 124

Keep File in Memory startup option, 99
Keep Lines Together paragraph option, 87
Keep Program in Memory startup option, 99
Keep With Next ¶ paragraph option, 86
Keys commands option, 22–23

landscape print orientation, 81
LaserWriter printers, 16
  cover pages with, 102
  Page Setup dialog box for, 81
  Page Setup options for, 82
  Print dialog box for, 101
  printing back to front with, 102
  selecting paper source for, 100–101
  selecting paper types for, 80
  shadowed text with, 121
leaders, setting, 87
Left paragraph option, 86
letters, lowercase,
  designating paragraphs, 108–109
  for section page numbers, 118
letters, uppercase, 11
  designating paragraphs, 108–109
  hyphenation with, 56
  matching, 35
  for section page numbers, 118
  spell checking of words with, 128
line numbering
  options for, 31, 86, 118
  in sections, 118
Line Numbering paragraph option, 86
Line Numbers section option, 118
Line Spacing ruler icons, 124
lines
  counting, 139–140
  dashed/solid, 87
  spacing between, 124
linked information, 90–91, 138
  hidden identifiers, 91
List commands option, 22
List formula options, 43
logical operators, used in print merges, 104

MacPaint files, 70
MacWrite (Claris) files, 70, 115
MacWrite files, 70
mail messages, 73–74, 120
Mail (Microsoft), 73, 141, 142
mailing labels, printing, 105
Make Backup save option, 113
Manual Feed print option, 101
Margin icon, 106
margins
  indenting, 86
  justifying, 124
  resetting with Print Preview, 106
  setting, 29–30
Margins document option, 29
mathematical formulas
  commands and options, 41–45
  creating, 41
  showing/hiding, 41
  viewing, 54
mathematical operations, 7–8, 137
memory
  document files loaded in, 99
  program files loaded in, 99
Menu commands option, 22
Merge Cells table option, 132
merging
  cells, 132

form letters, 103–105
Microsoft Excel, 91
Microsoft Mail, 73, 141, 142
Microsoft QuickSwitch Utility, 90–91
printing text, 101
Update Link command with, 138
Microsoft RTF format, 70, 114, 115
Microsoft Word 1.0 file conversion, 114
Microsoft Word 3.0
file conversion to, 115
importing text into tables, 65
Microsoft Word 4.0
installing Symbol character set with, 41, 45
listing commands, 23
loading files into system's memory, 99
networking, 141–143
online help for, 52–53
quitting, 107
site license for, 143
Microsoft Word 4.0 (DOS) files, 115
Microsoft Word 5.0 (DOS) files, 115
Microsoft Word User's Guide, online help references to, 52
Microsoft Works
converting files to, 114
opening files from, 70
Microsoft Write 3.0, converting files to, 115
Minimum Row Height cells option, 10
minus or subtraction sign (-)
as mathematical operator, 8
for removing words from dictionary, 128
used with Oulining command, 76, 77
Mirror Even/Odd Margins document option, 29–30
modems transmission, formatting file for, 114
MS-DOS files, 115
MultiFinder, 59, 90
multiplication symbol (*), 8

Nested index option, 58
New Column section option, 117
New command (File menu), 68
New Page section option, 117
New Window command (Window menu), 69
newspaper-style columns, 19–20
Next Column cells option, 10
Next File document option, 31
No Break section option, 117
Normal Paragraph ruler icon, 125
Number of Columns table option, 65
Number From document option, 31
Number Lines From document option, 31
Number Pages From document option, 30
Number of Rows table option, 65
numbering. *See* line numbering; page numbering; paragraph numbering

Odd Page section option, 117
odd-numbered pages, starting section on, 117
Open Space ruler icons, 124
Open command (File menu), 70–71
Open Documents with Ruler startup option, 125
Open File Name command, 23
Open Footer command (Document menu), 72
Open Header command (Document menu), 72
Open Mail command (File menu), 73–74
Open command option, 23
Orientation print option, 80–81
Outline command (Format menu), 75
Outline icon bar, 76–77
outlined characters, 75, 102
outlines, 76–79
creating table of contents from, 133
printing, 102
Outlining command (Document menu), 76–79, 137
for defining paragraph levels, 109
Outside Bar border option, 5
Outside position option, 95
Overstrike formula command, 44

Page Break Before paragraph option, 86
page breaks
before new section, 117
before paragraphs, 86
manual, 111
preventing, 87, 117
repaginating, automatic, 111
repositioning of, with Print Preview, 106
page icon, 72
Page Number icon, 106
page numbers/page numbering
automatic, 72

format of, in sections, 117–118
in headers/footers, 72
mirroring, 106
positioning of, with Print Preview, 106
starting, 30
in table of contents, 133
Page Setup command (File menu), 80–83
Page Setup warning box, 16
Page View command (Document menu), 19–20, 84, 98
pages
moving to, 51
positioning text or graphics on, 94–96
starting sections on even-numbered, 117
starting sections on odd-numbered, 117
Pages/Page Range print option, 100
paper
for ImageWriters, 80
for LaserWriters, 80
selecting default sizes of, 99
source of, 100–101
Paper page setup option, 80
Paper Source print option, 100–101
Paragraph command (Format menu), 85–88
paragraph numbering, 108–110
Paragraph Width position option, 96
paragraphs
borders for, 4–5, 88
counting, 139–140
formatting options for, 85–88
formatting when printing in draft mode, 102
menu of styles for, 124
restoring to default style of, 125
setting width of, 96
space before, 124
style sheets for, 26–27
styling, 129–130
widow control, 31
Paragraphs numbering option, 108
parentheses
in arrays, 41
in calculations, 8
in Displace formula command, 42
Paste command (Edit menu), 7, 24, 89
Paste Link command (Edit menu), 90–91
pasting
graphic images, 89
information from other applications, 90–91
text, 89
percentage symbol (%), 8
placeholders for graphic images, 98
Plain for Style command (Format menu), 92
Plain Text command (Format menu), 3, 67, 75, 93
plain text (ASCII) files, 71, 114
plus or addition sign (+)
as mathematical operator, 8
used to add words to dictionary, 128
used with Outlining command, 76, 77
point size, 5, 14, 97
portrait print orientation, 81
ports for printers, 16
Position character option, 14
Position command (Format menu), 94–96
Position paragraph option, 88
PostScript files
printing codes for, 101
printing over text, 82
Preferences command (Edit menu), 29, 61, 97–99, 137
Prev. Column cells option, 10
Preview position option, 96
Print Back to Front print option, 102
Print command (File menu), 31, 100–102
Print Hidden Text print option, 98, 101
Print Merge command (File menu), 103–105
Print Next File print option, 101
print orientation, 80–81
Print PostScript Over Text print option, 82
Print Preview command (File menu), 19–20, 96, 106
Print Selection Only print option, 101
print spoolers, 142–143
printers
for borders, 6
customizing paper size for, 99
networking, 141–143
page setup options, 80–83
selecting, 15–16
printing
back to front, 102
creating print queue, 31
documents, 100–102
hairline borders, 6

number of copies, 100
pausing, 101
quality, 102

Quality print option, 102
QuickSwitch Utility (Microsoft), 90–91, 118
printing of text for, 101
Quit command (File menu), 107
quotation marks ("), printing typeset-quality, 98

Radical formula command, 44
radical (root) sign, 44
Redo command (Edit menu), 137
Reduce or Enlarge page setup option, 82
reducing documents, 82
Renumber command (Utilities menu), 108–110
Repaginate Now command (Document menu), 111, 137
repaginating. *See* page numbering
replacing text after search, 11
resizing
characters, resetting, 92
graphic images, 59–60
Restart Each Section document option, 31
revealing codes, 54–55
Rich Text Format (RTF), 70, 114, 115
Right paragraph option, 86
Roman numerals
for paragraphs, 108–110
for section page numbers, 118
rows
cell height in, 10
converting table to text, 135
creating, in tables, 65
modifying, 131–132
RTF (Rich Text Format), 70, 114, 115
ruler, 123–125
Run-in index option, 58

Same as Previous header/footer option, 72
Save As command (File menu), 18, 112–115
Save As command option, 23
Save command (File menu), 112–115
saving,
command configuration files, 33
document options as default, 31
documents, 112–115
glossaries, 48
page setup options as default, 82
position settings, 96
section options as default, 117
styles, 127
scale, 125
Scale ruler icon, 125
scaling graphic images, 59–60
Scrapbook, 59
searching, 35
and replacing, 11
Section command (Format menu), 30, 116–119
Section Range print option, 101
sections
formatting, 116–119
printing, 101
semicolon (;), in index entries, 61
Send Mail command (File menu), 120
separator characters, for numbering paragraphs, 109
Set Default document option, 31
Set Default page setup option, 82
Shadow command (Format menu), 121
shadowed characters, 121
Shift Cells table option, 132
Short Menus, versus Full Menus, 145
Short Menus command, 46
Show ¶ command (Edit menu), 54–55
Show Clipboard command (Window menu), 122
Show Hidden Text option, 61, 66, 98
Show Ruler command (Format menu), 123–125
Show Table Gridlines setup option, 98
Show Text Boundaries in Page View setup option, 98
single spacing, 86, 124
Size character option, 13
"Smart" Quotes setup option, 98
snaking columns, 19–20
Sort command (Utilities menu), 126
sorting, 126
space
before paragraphs, 124
between columns, 10, 19, 65
between margin and row, 10
right edge of page to page number, 118
setting around text or graphic image, 95
top edge of page to page number, 118
underlining, 13

white, 5
Space Between Cols cells option, 10
spacing
between characters, 14
between paragraphs, 86
double, 124
of numbers in arrays, 42
single, 86, 124
special characters. *See also* hidden characters
hidden, 61
hiding/showing, 54–55
spelling check, 127–128
Spelling command (Utilities menu), 68, 71, 127–128, 137
Split Cell table option, 132
Start At number option, 108
Start section option, 117
strings. *See* character string searches
Style options for formatting text, 14
Style Selection Box on ruler, 124
style sheets
merging, 71
modifying, 26–27
Open command with, 71
printing, 102
styles
automatic, 130
of paragraphs, 129–130
Styles command (Format menu), 129–130
subscript characters, 14, 93
in formulas, 44
units of measurement of, 97
subtraction or minus sign (–)
as mathematical operator, 8
for removing words from dictionary, 128
used with Outlining command, 76, 77
Superscript/Subscript command, 44
superscript characters, 14, 93
in formulas, 44
units of measurement of, 97
Symbol character set, 41, 45
symbols
in footnotes, 39
in formulas, 41
for integral operations, 43
for mathematical operations, 8
system memory. *See* memory
System 7 (Macintosh OS), 28

Tab Delimited table option, 65
tab stops
default, 31
icons on ruler, 124
marks showing, 103
setting, 87–88
Table command (Edit menu), 131–132
table of contents
compiling, 133–134
Next File option for, 31
printing codes, 101
selecting text for, 66
Table of Contents command (Utilities menu), 133–134
Table scale, 125
Table to Text command (Document menu), 135
tables. *See also* cells; columns
borders for, 4, 5–6
converting rows to text, 135
creating and formatting, 64–65
gridlines in, 98
importing text into, 65
modifying, 131–132
Tabs options, 87–88
tag lines, 39
text. *See also* documents
comma-delimited, 65
controlling placement on page, 94–95
copying, 24
cutting, 25
deleting, 17
hiding, 77
inserting, 89
printing extra-high quality, 82
resetting enhancements to, 92
tab-delimited, 65
Text Only save option, 114
Text Only With Line Breaks save option, 114
Text Smoothing page setup option, 82
text strings. *See* character string searches
time
in documents, 48
in header or footer, 72
transmission, formatting files for, 114

Underline command (Format menu), 136
Underline character option, 13
underlining, 13, 136
underscoring, 42
Undo command (Edit menu), 137
units of measurement, 97

Update Link command (Edit menu), 90, 138
Use Picture Placeholders setup option, 98

version command, 1
vertical bars, 87, 124
Vertical line ruler icon, 124
Vertical position option, 95
viewing
    files, 70
    formatting changes, 12
    formulas, 41
    hidden text, 61, 66, 98
    newspaper-style columns, 19
    with Print Preview, 106

white space. *See* space
Widow Control document option, 31
widows, 31
Width of Column cells option, 10
windows, 69
Word. *See* Microsoft Word
Word Count command (Utilities menu), 139–140
words
    counting, 139–140
    finding in several documents, 35, 36
    searching, 11
    underlining, 13

Keystroke Commands

Command	Keystroke Sequence
Again	⌘-A
All Caps	⌘-Shift-K
Bold	⌘-Shift-B
Calculate	⌘-=
Change	⌘-H
Change Font	⌘-Shift-E
Character	⌘-D
Close	⌘-W
Copy	⌘-C
Cut	⌘-X
Decrease Font Size	⌘-Shift-<
Define Styles	⌘-T
Dotted Underline	⌘-Shift-\
Double Underline	⌘-Shift-[
Find	⌘-F
Find Again	⌘-Option-A
Footnote	⌘-E
Glossary	⌘-K
Go Back	⌘-Option-Z
Go To	⌘-G
Help	⌘-?
Hidden Text	⌘-Shift-X
Increase Font Size	⌘-Shift->
Insert Index Entry	⌘-Option-I
Insert Line Break	Shift-Return
Insert New Section	⌘-Return
Insert Page Break	Shift-Enter
Italics	⌘-Shift-I